HOW TO *Lose* SOMEONE

CW00550691

AND FIND
THE
Beautiful
IN THE
AWFUL

NATALIE HAYNES

Acorn & Athena Publishing

TABLE OF CONTENTS

1

INTRODUCTION

My dad died. And as of the start of this writing, now I'm helping my mom in her years with dementia. I've also started more closely recognizing other forms of loss and finding moments and relationships that are beautiful and meaningful, even in loss. *Especially* in loss.

This is my story about what I've learned about loss of various kinds. I was directly responsible for only some of these.

I want to share my experiences because it might help someone cry or laugh right when you need it.

I'm sorry you're reading this, because if you are that means you're probably going through a loss or expecting one. My hope is to help you, even if it's just to make you laugh or to make you feel like you're not alone in how it feels to lose someone or something, physically, mentally, or emotionally.

I lost my father in 2018. As it happened, I took a lot of notes on the ridiculous moments, amusing moments, and the decisions that my family made. We made some great decisions, but we were a textbook example of being under-prepared. The good news is that, no matter what level of preparation you have, even if you skipped something, it's going to be ok.

Someone might die, but other than that, it's going to be ok.

We didn't plan ahead for anything. When my father got sick, we thought he would make a full recovery. He worked out regularly, ate well, and was healthy for seventy-seven years. And then suddenly he wasn't.

His heart's mitral valve tendon snapped. Consequences of that are that the heart can still beat, but you eventually feel like you're drowning in the fluid building in your lungs. It feels like that because that is what happens.

He was sick for ten weeks before he passed.

The blessing of having ten weeks is that our family at least had time to say what we needed to say. I'm not sure if it's better to lose someone quickly like a car crash or very slowly like someone battling cancer for years or somewhere in the middle like my dad's situation. I do not like any of these options, but I can't wish my experience away as something different, so I choose to be grateful for those ten weeks exactly as they are.

I lost my dad fairly quickly, and now I'm slowly losing my mom.

Don't worry, I can still make it funny. Or try to.

I have slid into the role of being a caregiver for her, a maintenance worker, and a leader of the household. I have to find the humor in the awful to absorb it. And I grasp at straws sometimes when I'm trying to be grateful for any of it. I want to share about this, because so many of us will go through the process of helping someone in their last years, weeks, and days. Often it involves great sacrifice. Often it is not something that anyone else truly sees.

Experiencing my losses has taught me to be more aware of the losses of others, so that is part of my story here too.

I am certainly not here to preach about the right way to do anything. I'm just sharing my story from my heart.

Also, we take a left turn or two at the end. So buckle up, buttercup!

2

COME HOME

I live in San Francisco, California, but I'm from Birmingham, Alabama. My family still lives in the same redbrick two story house that I grew up in. Ivy vines rope up the sides of the trees. There's a small garden patio beside the house where the wisteria drapes over the bushes in the spring and where we sit and talk and watch fireflies at night. The wisteria is purple and smells sweet. The fireflies usually start in May and last into July.

In March, I woke up to a text from my cousin Maggie saying "You need to come home. Your dad is in the ICU."

I took the next flight available and went straight to the hospital to join my mom, Maggie, her husband Eric, and Maggie's mom Dotsy, all gathered around my dad.

My father was intubated because he couldn't breathe on his own. Since having a tube down your throat is uncomfortable, they sedated him, so he was unconscious.

Talking to myself:

Of course he's not going to die.

He might die.

No.

What if he does die?

No. He'll be fine. He's healthy. He's fine. I'm fine. Mom is fine. Everyone is going to be fine.

...Did I even get my suitcase at baggage claim?

I need a glass of wine. Why does this hospital not serve wine?

Apparently, hospitals generally don't serve wine. Especially at 10am.

Lesson: You have to bring your own wine to the hospital.

With my suitcase, my mom and I, both completely stunned, left the hospital and drove home.

At home, a neighbor had left bagels and cream cheese for us in a bag on our doorstep.

It was the first of many kindnesses.

3

IS IT TIME TO PANIC?

Years ago, I travelled frequently with a very good friend, and inevitably, we occasionally ran into extremely frustrating travel challenges. We developed a rule: Only one person gets to panic at a time. And we took turns on who kept it together.

I was still feeling out whether it was Mom or me that gets to panic now. For the most part, I think both of us were acting like this is all just normal. Or that it's not even real. No panicking.

Dad is in the ICU, but clearly this isn't really a problem. This isn't happening. Nothing is wrong. Do you want eggs for breakfast? I'm making eggs.

Eventually I had to address the situation though.

This IS happening. It IS real. And everything IS wrong.

I know how to take a challenging situation and execute a plan. But first you have to understand the problem. I understood nothing here. In the beginning, all I knew was that my dad wasn't able to talk to us, he looked like he was about to die, my mother was exhibiting "childlike behavior", as one of the nurses put it, so any detailed conversation needed to go through me.

I HAVE to keep it together. I DON'T get to fall apart right now. It is NOT my turn.

Breathe. NOT MY TURN.

My thoughts at the hospital: What's happening? Will he be ok? What caused this? What can we do to help him to be ok? When is he going to be off the ventilator? When can he talk again? When can he come home? What are next steps? Why are these machines making noises? What are all the numbers on the screens? Is that number good? Is something wrong? It seems to be beeping faster now... yeah it's definitely not in normal range now... because now I know what normal range is... I know because now we've been here for three weeks. I hate that I know how to read the machines.

And then we're talking about his wishes:

ICU Nurse: Does he have an Advanced Medical Directive?

Me: What? I've never heard of this. Mom, does he have that?

Mom: I don't know.

Me: Does he have a will?

Mom: I don't know.

Me: Umm, do you have a will?

Mom: I don't know.

Me: (Quiet for a while...while the machines are beeping) Do you know where the deed to the house is?

Mom: No.

Me: The titles to the cars?

Mom: I'm not sure.

Me: (Thinking, thinking... with the beeping) Do you have a box at the bank?

Mom: I don't know.

To my credit, I didn't curse out loud in that moment.

What I did do is go home and rip up my dad's office looking for any of these documents.

We call his office the "garage apartment", because it was originally built to be an apartment and it's over the garage (clever name for it, yes?). My point in explaining that is that it's a seperate dwelling and bigger than a normal one-room office at home, so searching took two weeks of sorting through files and piles of papers saved for over forty years on two levels of what would normally be a living space plus an attic.

I also didn't want my mom to see me doing all of this in a wild near-panic (because... NOT MY TURN), so I did it all after she went to sleep.

I found things like the manual for the VCR we had in 1985, receipts for $2 glue from K-Mart which were part of a tax write-off for home improvement, and sweet cards that Dad and Mom exchanged when they were first married.

But I found nothing helpful for legal purposes.

I did however burn all the documents I didn't need out in the yard in an aluminum barrel (not the sweet cards).

Just after starting the fire, I got a text from the neighbor saying that there was a fire at my mom's house. She thought I was in California. I texted back, "Thank you, but everything is fine. I started the fire, and I have a fire extinguisher and a hose right beside me, so it's intentional and safe."

Too late.

The next thing I see is a fire truck coming down the street and a dozen firefighters coming up the driveway.

I might have otherwise welcomed a firefighter at my house at 10pm, but in that moment I was mad that they woke up my mom and scared her.

I restarted the fire when they left.

4

THE FIVE PRIORITIES

I don't think there's a "right" way to manage a sick parent. But here's how I did it.

Every morning I woke up and thought, "What are my priorities today?"

In order, the five priorities:

- Dad
- Mom
- The house
- Legal things
- Me

DAD: Mom and I took turns spending time with him at the hospital. My mom was a most devoted and loving wife. She got dressed up very cute every day and stayed right next to him early in the day. I visited in the evenings and tried to stay with him until he went to sleep. I worked with him on physical therapy which he needed in order to regain the ability to walk. Walking was a requirement before the cardiac surgeon would operate. Dad needed to be strong enough to walk before he'd be strong enough to endure the surgery, so I did resistance training with him.

MOM: She stayed really positive and strong, but I was always wondering how she was feeling about Dad being in the hospital.

If she was scared or upset, she didn't talk about it.

She was also forgetting things more than I'd ever noticed before. At the time I wrote it off as being due to stress.

THE HOUSE: My first day at home, the refrigerator was loudly rattling. This was just the start of many necessary maintenance issues I noticed around the house. My favorite maintenance moment, though, was when I asked my mom why she wasn't using the dishwasher. She couldn't remember, so I tested the dishwasher to see if it worked. And it worked just fine. What didn't work was the output pipe, so all the water from the dishwasher rained into the basement through the floorboards. It was comically bad. I'm an only child, and I've never wanted a sibling more than I did in that moment. I would have just turned my head to communicate in a glance, "This is what we're dealing with. A whole effing house full of this kind of thing."

My second favorite maintenance moment was the first day it rained (real rain this time, not dishwasher rain), and I walked in to find my mom watching TV with pots around her.

Me: What is going on? Why are there pots all over the sunporch?

Mom: Well, the ceiling is leaking, but it's ok, I fixed it with the pots.

Me (trying not to laugh or otherwise make her feel bad): Yeah, that's good. We probably also need to find another way to fix it.

Thankfully when I was going on my paper riffling rampage in my dad's office, I had taken notes on who he used for professional services (electrical, plumbing, etc.), so I knew to call Oswaldo for roof things. Oswaldo eventually fixed the roof for us.

I found it really helpful to make a list of people to call, including neighbors, friends, service people like Oswaldo, trash pickup, doctors, lawyers... I printed all of that for my mom and left it on the refrigerator. I also keep a running list in an online file that I share with my cousins. In case something happens to me, someone else can help my mom.

LEGAL THINGS: As I said above, I woke up thinking about five things. It would have been nice to only manage four or three. I would have had more bandwidth to take care of the people that I love, rather than dealing with paperwork and house issues. We did take care of all of the legal things, but we scrambled to do it, and it wasn't thoughtfully planned. We improved it later, but the first round was only adequate, not ideal.

Lesson: The two things you can handle early are legal things and house maintenance.

And then there's priority #5.

ME: "Take care of yourself." Right. This is well-intentioned advice. However, in the moment, my thoughts were: Dad is in the hospital, Mom is not quite herself, and the refrigerator is making strange loud noises, and people keep calling, and I have a job interview at two p.m. which I'm going to need to take from some empty room in the ICU, and we're also out of cat food, and did I even eat today?, and Mom needs me to write instructions on how to use the thermostat for the house, and she also needs a cell phone so I can call her at the hospital, and did she eat today? When is trash day? Is that dead tree about to fall on the house? People brought food, and we need to label it and also send thank you notes. When the fuck do I have time to take care of myself? Would that be before I picked my mom up out of the bathtub when she fell, or after washing out my dad's spit cup filled with blood at the hospital? It's a good day if I even take a shower.

Do I have a career anymore? What is happening? Is he going to die? What if he doesn't die and he sees what I did to his office while I was looking for the papers? Who needs me right now? Do we still need to find a notary for our meeting on Tuesday? Is that toilet supposed to make that noise?

All of those thoughts are real. Obviously, you try to cope and prioritize, but of my five priorities, I made myself the last. I felt guilty for even thinking of myself. Am I going to go to the gym while my dad is in the hospital? Getting a manicure? No. Maybe other people do, and maybe I should have, but I couldn't. Or I didn't. I readily admit that I am not always a shining example of the best way to do things.

A lot of people have compared this situation to the instructions they give on airplanes which is to put your own mask on to help yourself before you help someone else. I am sure that's great advice on an airplane. Except even on an airplane, I'd help my parent before myself and hold my breath. And that's exactly what it felt like. Holding my breath.

And part of taking care of myself was not judging myself for holding my breath. I did what I thought was right.

5

SQUEEZE MY HAND

My dad was unconscious at first, and even when he came back to being aware of everything, he still couldn't talk. I know he could understand us because his eyes were alert, and when the surgeon told us that he needed to be walking before they would operate, Dad started wiggling his feet. I am sure Dad knew everything we were saying, but he couldn't talk for at least a week. We ended up holding his hand and asking him yes/no questions so that we could say "if you want more blankets, squeeze my hand, yes." "If you want it cooler, squeeze my hand, yes." Given the circumstances, this worked well.

We also did this with legal things since I hadn't found any of the legal documents in his office. Two family friends worked with an attorney to write a will for my father which was brought to the hospital ICU waiting room. Without others in the room, I asked Dad if he trusted the people who were helping us. He squeezed "yes". Since that day, those two people have become like second fathers to me.

I'm not a lawyer, and this is not official legal advice, just my notes.

My advice is to get everything in order early. A few things to look into or note:

- Talk about end-of-life wishes.
- Have a will.
- Know where all of the important family documents are, and tell several people.
- Consider an AMD - Advanced Medical Directive. E.g. Do you want to be on a ventilator or feeding tube? Do you want CPR? For an elderly person, CPR often breaks ribs. Some people opt out of that. These documents are state-specific.
- Set up a trust. It protects the assets for the family and prevents real estate from going through probate which is complicated, lengthy, and expensive. Trusts are not just for rich people.
- Periodically revisit the beneficiary designations on financial accounts.
- Consider arranging Power of Attorney for both financial and medical issues. Important note: Powers of Attorney are only applicable while the person is alive.

We did none of these things ahead of time, and consequently I spent my time with lawyers when I would rather have been with my family.

The good news though, is that it all got done, and even if you haven't planned ahead, you can deal with it. But taking care of these things early will only make it easier on you during a difficult time.

6

THE NET THAT CATCHES YOU

I didn't sleep much when my dad was sick.

But one day I woke up to the sound of lawn mowers. I looked outside to see several men from our church in our yard on their riding lawn mowers, while several of their wives helped in the garden. It was also 100 degrees in a humid Alabama summer. If there's any way to shine love on a struggling family, they found it.

We had many moments of love like that, and after that very first day with the bagels on our doorstep, I started keeping a book of gratitude. I wrote down everything that anyone did for us. The book was partly to make sure we wrote thank you notes, partly to remember, and partly to look back and know that as much hurt as we have, we also have a lot to be thankful for. And we are thankful.

One of the other early kindnesses was so simple, but I will never forget it.

Coming off the ventilator, my dad woke up. And one of the first things on his mind was that he had a library book that needed to be returned.

ARE YOU KIDDING ME? You just came back to consciousness from being nearly dead and a library book is what you're worried about?!

At least his mind was sharp. It was really important to him to get that book returned.

So when Dan, a man I'd never met, from my parents' Sunday school class called and asked if there was anything he could do for us, I said "Yes! Can you please return a library book for me? I'm too tired to drive anywhere." I hate asking for help or inconveniencing someone for something so small, but I needed help.

I had to just start letting people help. I surrendered and said yes.

The net that catches you.

Other kindnesses: Many people brought us food. And it was all delicious, but I learned about Tomato Pie. If you're not familiar with this Southern delicacy, think of a quiche, but with a lot of tomatoes, butter, mayonaise, onion, basil, and cheese. Holy smokes, it's good.

People at the church started a schedule for all the food they were planning to bring so that we didn't end up with five gallons of chicken salad on one day. Someone somewhere was very organized. I don't even know who to thank for that. I am simply grateful.

In the South, casseroles are the currency of love sometimes.

There is absolutely no way I can recount all the kind things that people have done for our family, so my intention here is to simply share some of the funny moments.

My cousin Loxley came over to help me one day with cleaning out the attic at the office. This is in a 100-plus-degree humid Alabama summer heat, and we were facing quite a task in cleaning and removing

17

everything in the attic including old furniture. After a bit of deliberation on how to get things down a delicate foldable attic staircase and then around multiple corners and additional stairs, we decided instead to cut out a window screen in the attic and just throw things out of the window. We had to clean it up later of course, but we had a GREAT TIME.

While I was doing all of this cleaning, I was also visiting my dad every day. And on one of the first days he was back to consciousness, he was groggy but said,

Dad: Nat, what day is it?

Me: Sunday

Dad: No, I mean what DATE is it?

Me: It's Sunday, April 8th.

Dad: So we have a week.

Me: Ummm [pause, to marvel at what I think he means]. Do you mean we have a week FOR TAXES?

Dad: Yeah

Oh my gosh. The man nearly died and this was one of the first things on his mind upon being responsive again. Taxes and a library book. He can hardly get a full sentence out, but he never missed a beat on being responsible.

I had taken care of the taxes by then. I am so thankful that I had a father who taught me to take care of things like that. Planning ahead for yourself is part of the net that catches you too.

7

DANNY & B

While I was in Alabama dealing with my dad, I had an 18 year old cat in California that also needed help. Thank the heavens for Danny. Danny is my best friend and neighbor, and my cat, Mr. B, loved him.

While I was with my family, Danny checked on B.

One day, Danny said, "I don't think B is going to make it much longer."

B couldn't stand up anymore. He was suffering.

My dad was in the ICU. My cat was essentially in cat ICU at home. Obviously my dad is more important, but I still booked the next flight to San Francisco in order to put B down at home, with hugs, in comfort.

You know how some flights are just perfect, and the timing works out exactly as planned? Not this time! The phrase "hell in a handbasket" comes to mind for this trip. During my layover, we were on the plane, then off the plane, then re-routed to another plane, then directed to re-book with the gate agent. In the middle of that, Danny called to tell me that I could cancel the euthanasia visit. So of course, I'm now silently crying at the Denver airport while waiting in line.

My dad is maybe dying. My cat is dead. Why am I even trying to go to California now? Some angel miracle woman saw my silent tears and somehow got me on the next flight so I could at least get to my cat. I don't know her name. I don't know what she did. But she helped me. And I got home.

I walked into my apartment, and Danny was there waiting for me. By this time I was done with crying, so I didn't cry when I saw B laid out on the floor right where he died.

That cat was really dead. I wanted to hug him, but he was like a rock. I sat on the floor gently petting my dead cat and looked up at Danny and said, "Well, what are we going to do with him?"

Both of us -- wide eyed, looking "I don't know".

We're not going to throw him away. We can't compost him...

Let's put him in the freezer and worry about this later.

And so we did that. We double bagged the dead cat and then put him in an empty freezer. And then we went for drinks around the corner. Because it was THAT kind of day.

8

MANAGING COMMUNICATIONS

One of the blessings of having so many people care about my father was that many people wanted to know if he was ok. People called us a lot to check on him. One older friend in particular used to call us at six a.m. frequently.

We didn't have time to answer all the phone calls and emails. Instead I sent out a weekly email update to family and friends. That was a great way to stay connected to everyone, to express gratitude and to communicate when Dad did and didn't want visitors. I also took that opportunity to tell brief stories about things he'd said or done that were amusing. He liked making people laugh.

One day, I breezed into his hospital room for 30 seconds and asked my mom if she'd had lunch. I started to leave to get her some soup, and Dad asked where I was going so fast. I said I was getting lunch for Mom. He merrily said "Ok... I'll be here." It was his way of joking about the fact that he couldn't eat or walk. This was in the earlier hospital days.

This was also before Mom and I agreed that it was cruel to eat and drink in front of him since he couldn't.

In addition to stories about my dad, I also told stories about myself in the emails. For example, in my efforts to help around the house, I'd been watering all the plants. Eventually I noticed that at least five of them were artificial plants.

9

BEING AT THE HOSPITAL

My father spent nine weeks in the hospital and one at home.

We saw a lot of sad and worried people in the ICU. At least we weren't sad. In fact, we laughed a lot. I don't remember what we were laughing about, but I sometimes felt bad that we might be making other people feel worse because we laughed so much.

I think we were less somber than others because none of us thought he was really dying.

But eventually the laughing stopped. He was getting depressed. One day I asked why he never watched TV at the hospital, and he said he didn't want to watch people doing things he can't do.

I never ate or drank anything in front of him after that.

We'd all been there too long.

You know when you've been at the hospital too much when you know which vending machines are working and when you start giving other people directions on how to get into the ICU after normal hours. There are a lot of things like this, that I wish I didn't know.

- I wish I didn't know which hospital doors will open after one a.m.
- I wish I didn't know the labyrinth of the hospital hallways, which bathrooms are nicer, and the hours of the cafeteria. Soup is on the right side of the room, and sandwiches are on the left.
- I also wish the surgeon would just operate, which is what my dad wants, even though his chances are 50/50 to survive. The alternative is 100% to not survive.
- I wish the surgeon wasn't evaluated on success rates, because then he could take on what he called a "risky patient".
- I wish I'd known to demand antidepressants for Dad.
- I wish I'd been a better advocate for him.
- I wish I didn't know the hospital smell.

My dad wished to die rather than stay in the hospital. He asked me to kill him several times. I tried to encourage him, and I brought inspirational pictures from his office. But he was normally a very energetic and active person, so lying in bed 24 hours a day for nine weeks was unbearable for him. Eventually, there was no joy left.

10

PEPPERMINT AND BUTTERSCOTCH

One day after Dad was able to speak again, he was mustering the energy to say something very important.

One word at a time, he said, "... Nat.... I .... need............. peanut butter." This made me smile. I was expecting something a little more important at the end of that sentence, but it was important to him to ask for food.

Over time, he was increasingly upset about not being able to eat anything. So after two months of his being in the hospital and not eating, I made an executive decision. He couldn't eat peanut butter, a hamburger, or a bowl of ice cream (all of which he asked for), but they were letting him have ice chips. Why not let him at least have some slivers of candy? He loved peppermint and butterscotch, so what the hell. Give the man some candy. I went down to his workshop at home and took a hammer to several pieces of candy and brought it to him at the hospital. And I brought him a little melted ice cream too. He wasn't supposed to have any food because they said he couldn't swallow solid food without choking, but I wish I'd thought to do this sooner with the candy and ice cream. He didn't choke, and he was so happy.

The next morning I woke up to the phone ringing at 5:30, and I was annoyed thinking that it was that family friend who usually calls at six a.m. Mom took the call, and it wasn't our friend. It was Dad asking for me. I immediately called him back to make sure he was OK, since he had never used the hospital phone to call anyone before. He beat around the bush for a while, but eventually he said, "Hey, um, could you bring me some more... treats?"

Treats. His new code word. I always brought treats after that.

He was really funny about the treats, because he was afraid of getting in trouble with the doctors. He said, "What if they catch us? I might get kicked out of here". I told him "You've been trying to get out of here for weeks! I think it's fine. Just blame it on me if anyone asks."

He finally had some joy back.

Unfortunately, it was not enough.

11

GOING HOME

Being in the hospital for over two months was agony for Dad. One day, Dad reached for my hand and emotionally apologized to me for giving up. He desperately wanted to go home.

He wasn't getting better mentally or physically anyway. So I said, "Ok. Let's get you out of here."

My hope was that being home would help him get stronger and make him happier, but I also knew it was basically suicide to leave the hospital for very long. He knew that too. It was his last chess move.

He was home the next day.

They did not send the medical equipment necessary to drain his lungs, which he still needed, but we didn't know that until days later.

I thought hospice was going to help him medically, but they didn't. The hospital dumped him into an ambulance and into hospice care without sufficient food, wound care, or lung drainage.

They did give us morphine.

One smart choice we made was getting baby monitors for him. 24/7 we needed to hear what he needed, even with hospice. We kept two "parent" monitors around the house, and I called them the "intercom system" to preserve some dignity. I always had one with me, and we had one in the area where our hospice person was.

Another useful choice was writing the names of our hospice helpers down on a whiteboard for Dad so he, and we, knew who was taking care of him. The hospice workers changed shifts every eight hours. For each new person, I always greeted them, showed them around the house, and introduced them to Dad as a new "friend" who was there to help with things.

Mabel was the best.

Mabel was great with my dad, but she also took care of me and my mom. There was one day I was so tired. I was doing laundry, and I fell asleep under a pile of warm towels on my bed. I woke up with Mabel gently folding the towels and trying not to wake me up.

Mabel was also the nurse that was with my dad on his last day of being able to speak.

He told Mabel that he was going home tomorrow. Not knowing for certain what that meant, she asked if anyone else was going with him, and he said no.

He knew he was going to die.

12

THE INEVITABLE

Early one morning, the day before Dad died, Mom and I, both exhausted, were sitting on the sun porch and silently staring at the floor with our coffees. And then we saw a rabbit in the driveway that our cat had injured. The cat was sitting right beside the rabbit, just waiting to paw it again. I went outside and gently picked the rabbit up, brought it inside, and laid it in my lap to keep it away from the cat. We watched it breathe. I think Mom and I both needed it to live, just like we wanted Dad to stay with us. After breathing ten more minutes, it died right there.

"Whelp, I've got a dead rabbit in my lap now." We both laughed, knowing we both wanted to cry our hearts out.

Maybe this was a good way of preparing us in a small way for what was coming.

We buried the rabbit in the garden. And then we started planning Dad's funeral, while he was slowly dying upstairs. He had told Mabel that his favorite hymn was Amazing Grace, so we included that in the list of things to tell the church.

What flowers, what songs, what quotes, what Bible verses, when, where, how to tell people, who will speak, who will play the music, what pictures go on the bulletin. Can we host family at our house? Do we need to provide food after the service? Is the house clean? What should we wear?

It's like planning a wedding but there aren't any presents and everyone is sad.

13

A BEAUTIFUL DEATH

When the hospice service gives you morphine, they also give you a paper ledger in a binder. You're now a morphine accountant. Anything leaving the bottle needs to be recorded. You have to record the date, time, and amount every time morphine is administered.

We didn't touch the morphine until we had to.

Dad lost the ability to speak on Saturday, a few hours after the rabbit died. He had been home for eight days. He could still squeeze our hands though, and he looked into our eyes. I know he was still there then. We started squeezing three times to say "I love you". Three from me. And three back.

The next day, Sunday, was a beautiful day outside.

Inside, it was a little more complicated.

Dad was in his bedroom of forty-two years, and in the early evening the radiant sunset reds and oranges were shining through the leaves on the trees into his room. My mom and I held his hands and talked to him. He couldn't do "I love you" anymore. It was clearly getting harder for him to breathe. The fluid was building up in his lungs. We were all together. He was suffering, and Mom tearfully looked up at me and said "Natalie, please do something."

I stepped out of the room and called our relatives who are doctors, and they recommended giving him the maximum dosage of morphine per hour that was prescribed by the hospital doctor, because it would relieve any suffering and help him to move on.

And that's what I did.

Two hours later, his heart stopped, and he stopped breathing, without pain, holding our hands.

He got what he wanted. He was not in the hospital. He was at home with the people who loved him most.

I didn't break any laws. I followed the prescription precisely. I also stopped his suffering. And if anyone had to help him that way, I'm glad it was me.

14

THE LOGISTICS
OF DEATH

I'd like to say the rest of that night is a blur, but it isn't. With my dad dead on the bed, I was now focusing on my mom. The first thing for me was asking Mom if she wanted to spend time in the room with him. She didn't want to.

The next thing was helping her to leave that room. Then I called our neighbors, the Holleys, to ask them to please come be with her while I dealt with... I wasn't sure what yet.

I started with telling our hospice helper that we were not going to need her services for the rest of that night. And then I called the hospice service to make sure no one came the next day, or any other day.

And... who can come pick up my dad for cremation, and then when can someone come get the machines and the hospice bed?

I was on the phone for over an hour dealing with all of those things. I also called our closest family. While I was on the phone, neighbor Helen came upstairs and put a glass of wine in my hand. Bless her.

It took a few hours for the coroner's van to arrive. Eventually the Holleys had to leave. Mom and I sat in the living room. She was on a chair, and I sat on the floor next to her holding her hand. She was very composed the entire time but also stunned. She just said over and over, "I can't believe this is happening."

I'm grieving. She's grieving. I'm grieving that she's grieving.

What is she going to do? What am I going to do? Dad did everything around the house, and he took care of her. Who is going to … what should… how are we going to…. where do we… It's OK. It's OK. It's OK. Right now, we have to believe that it's OK. BREATHE BREATHE BREATHE.

I started asking myself -- Am I breathing? Yes. Am I in physical pain? No. Is Mom breathing? Yes. Is Mom in physical pain? No. Ok. Then just keep breathing.

You can't fix this one. OK. Breathe breathe.

I could only try to make it less awful for my mom.

They wrapped him in a green velvet blanket and carried him down the stairs. I told Mom not to look at that and instead talk to me, look at me. I didn't want that image to be her last memory of her husband.

And then he was really gone.

BREATHE. KEEP BREATHING.

We both tried to sleep, but I stayed up writing an update for the email list to let our friends and family know that he had passed.

One of the baby monitors was still on as I wrote. I heard Mom doing something upstairs around one a.m., and I was worried about how she must be feeling, so I went to her, and she was throwing up. She said, "Maybe I just drank too much."

No. She didn't drink too much. She lost her husband.

I was throwing up, too. I lost my dad.

Eventually we both calmed down enough to sleep.

15

PLANNING A WEDDING, I MEAN, A FUNERAL

Waking up the next day, the phone was ringing. My first thoughts flashed in a split second:

I think something bad happened.

Oh.

That.

No, no, please not that. Was that real? No. No. Please, no.

That is.

...

... is Mom OK?

Phone still ringing

Deal with it. Mom should not have to do anything right now.

The preacher was calling to help us with next steps.

He came over.

Thankfully after the rabbit died in my lap two days before, Mom and I already planned out a lot of the funeral decisions.

Mom was in shock. I'm not sure where I was emotionally. I was frustrated that we had to even plan a funeral right now.

I don't care about any of this. It's not going to bring him back. I will have to grieve seperately from this.

To me all of this was an inconvenient formality.

Slap some Amazing Grace on it, and let's get this over with. That's how I felt.

No one could have done anything differently to make it feel better than that to me. I didn't care about the hymns and the flowers. But Mom did. And other people did. And Dad deserved to be honored. And if we're going to do it, we should do it right. So of course I went along with the ceremony of it all.

I'm not going to sugarcoat anything though. I'm not having a "celebration of life" moment. I'm not celebrating life. I celebrated his life while he was here. Now I'm mourning a loss and officially assuming responsibility for many things. I miss my Dad, and it feels terrible, and I have to hold it together, because I am now the leader here.

IT IS STILL NOT MY TURN!

It's never going to be my turn to lose it, because if I stop juggling the balls, no one is going to pick them up. That's just not the phase we're in. No one is coming to take care of this, so I'm it.

My mom started calling me the CEO of the family. Accurate.

The preacher said someone had to write an obituary for the newspaper. I considered this to be completely useless, but my mom wanted it so, OK.

In my thankfully limited experience, I observed that the obituary business is ugly.

How much do you love your departed? Do you want the gold level obituary or just the aluminum level obituary? How about double platinum? How much will you spend?

How much will I spend?! Me? Not a damned thing if I can help it, and my father would have wanted it that way. And do not try to guilt trip me right now with your platinum level obituary package.

I wrote enough in the obituary to get the point across, honor my father, and keep my mom happy. No one reads the newspaper anymore anyway. I am grieving, and my priorities do not include trying to impress anyone with how much I loved my dad through how much I spent on an obituary. Spending LESS is actually what he'd want.

If we could write the obituary this way, he'd be exceptionally happy:

He died. Service: 2pm, Tuesday. [Church address].

I went with slightly more than that, but not much more.

Before the service at the church, I went to the ladies' room with my mom so we could collect ourselves. Then we went to the parlor to be with our close family. I joked that I might cry and that Dad would have been glad that I wasn't wearing expensive makeup. He was notoriously frugal. We all laughed. He would have wanted that (both the laughter and the inexpensive makeup).

I usually hate public speaking, but I wanted to tell my version of my dad. Below is my eulogy. Speaking these words is undoubtedly the hardest thing I've ever done. My cousin Loxley (from the day we threw things out of the window) stood next to me in case I couldn't get through it. I somehow maintained composure to say this:

> For those who don't know me, I'm Natalie Haynes, the daughter of Joe and Dottie Haynes.
>
> It is ok to be sad, but we are not here to be sad. We are here to be together. And we are here to celebrate a beautiful life. Thank you for being here. You are part of the fabric that is my dad's life.
>
> My father was born and raised on a small farm in East Tennessee, with his brother Jerry and sister Jeannie. Dad attended the U. S. Naval Academy at Annapolis, graduating in 1964. He then trained with some of the brightest minds in the world at the Navy's Nuclear Power School and Submarine School. During the cold war, he proudly served his country with several patrols aboard the USS Sam Rayburn, a Polaris missile nuclear submarine. In 1971, he graduated from Harvard Business School with honors.
>
> After that, he achieved his greatest accomplishment. He found my mom, Dottie, the love of his life.
>
> We still laugh about the fact that he used a coupon for dinner on their first date. Somehow, she still said yes when he asked to marry her just a few months later.
>
> Over the years, my dad told me many times that my mom is the best thing that ever happened to him. And I'm sure he's right.

My earliest memory of my dad is his reading me stories before I went to sleep. Our favorite book to read together was a classic, "Go Dog Go", which involved animals and general chaos, so we'd run around the room acting out what was happening in the book. I'm fairly sure my mom hated the "Go Dog Go" nights because it was not a book that made me sleepy.... But we sure had fun.

He was a really great father from the start.

My dad was an investor, a chemist, and a lifelong scholar. He tried to teach me algebra when I was 5. He also taught me to ride a bike, he put bandages on my knees, ---- AAAAND he also took really big bites out of my ice cream cones when we went to Dairy Queen. He really loved ice cream.

Another memory. When I was 10, a friend invited me to her birthday party at an ice skating rink. I didn't know how to ice skate, and I was really nervous about it. My dad saw that, so he took me to the ice skating rink to practice every day for two weeks. He helped me develop a plan to learn and to overcome my fears.... I definitely respect my father's other accomplishments, but in my opinion, THAT is the kind of thing that makes a man a real MAN.... He took care of me and my mom, and made us feel safe and strong.

My dad taught me that the most important things in life are not the things on your resume.

In addition to being a wonderful husband and father, my dad's life is also a testament to the importance of kindness, community, and friendship. One thought that has repeatedly come to me in the past few months is that "The measure of a man is his friendships". And as our family has gone through the past few months, LOVE has RAINED down upon us. Our family is absolutely humbled by the kindness that has met us in our moment of struggle, and now peace.

Joe Haynes always highly valued his faith, and our church family. Our family has been a part of this church and the Genesis Sunday School class for over 40 years. Dad lived his faith by action. He volunteered frequently and made a point of living a life of giving. He may have been frugal at times but he was generous when it mattered. He would never boast about the details, so I won't either, but I will say that when he saw a chance to make a difference, he did.

On the point of giving, I have two additional things to say:

1) First, Dad always had butterscotch in his pockets to give to the neighborhood kids and to the dog next door. We have butterscotch candy in baskets here, so please take one if you'd like to, as a celebration of kindness.

2) Second, in these circumstances, everyone wants to help, and no one knows what to do. So I'll give us all some words that he said to me: "Nat, when you can't sleep and you don't know what to do – think about what you're grateful for. Come to the day with positivity and gratitude and just do your best."

We can honor my father, Bobby Joe Haynes, by being grateful, by being our best selves, and by loving each other. That is what he would wish for all of us.

Thank you for being part of his life and for coming today. When it is time to leave this sanctuary, let us all go forth in gratitude, love, and with butterscotch in our pockets.

Neighbors Don and Helen Holley also spoke.

My cousin Loxley read a passage from the Bible.

The military salute at the end was touching. They presented the folded flag to my mom. It later ended up on the dining room table, and the cat slept on it for about a week.

I don't remember how we got to the church or back home. People just took care of us that day. The wonderful women from the church made sure to coordinate food at our house for a gathering after the service. I refuse to call it a party or celebration, but it was heartwarming to have my dad's Navy friends come over and tell us stories about the antics they had with him.

My dad's life makes me so proud to be his daughter. He had good friends. He was a good man.

OK, so the five priorities we talked about before were DAD, MOM, HOUSE, LEGAL, ME.

DAD is out of the list now. HOUSE and LEGAL are ok for now. That leaves MOM and ME.

Up next: MOM. While the Navy guys were downstairs sharing stories, my mom was changing clothes. It was taking longer than usual, so after 30 minutes I went up to see if she was OK. She was really focused on a blue shirt that she couldn't find. She said she thought that Jerry, Dad's brother, must have taken it. Jerry was staying in the garage apartment for the funeral weekend. Jerry wouldn't have taken a woman's shirt. He wouldn't have taken any shirt without asking. This, I wrote off as stress-induced confusion.

In the hospital, Dad had asked me to stay with Mom as long as I could. And that's what I've done. I think he knew she was developing dementia, but we never said that word.

16

WHAT PEOPLE SAY

Everyone meant well. But there are four phrases that I noted as things I will never say to another person going through loss.

1) He's in a better place.

> » Is he?
> » Why don't you go there then?

I keep a straight face, and I'm never feeling that I actually want that person dead, but those responses are exactly what I think, every time I hear this.

But I smile and nod and say thank you.

It's presumptive to think that the person losing someone has any specific spiritual beliefs.

I believe it would be better for him to be here with me and my mom. But thank you for your opinion on my dad's existence.

Those are the things I say to myself after smiling and nodding.

2) You'll be reunited with him one day.

I am happy for the people who do believe this, because the grief would perhaps be lessened. But I just don't think about death this way.

I have found peace in feeling that he isn't actually gone. He is with me always. We are not going to be able to hug each other, but I can still feel his love in what he taught me and how he treated me, and I see his spirit in his work. I feel Dad with me in many ways. I don't have to die to feel how much he loved me and see his enduring presence that I still love.

Again, I listen to the words people say. I smile and nod, and say thank you.

3) Everything happens for a reason.

> » Oh, really?
> » Why is he dead then? Do you ever question things?
> » How is this better? Who reasoned? What reason? Am I supposed to learn something? Is something better now?
> » What about Mom? Is she supposed to learn something? She doesn't seem better. We're both really sad and are adjusting to not having him.

For me, there is no reason. People just die sometimes. It doesn't have to make sense or be reasonable in any way.

All I can do now is try to take care of my mom and myself, and to muster the energy to bring something positive out of losing someone. For instance, I now call my Uncle Jerry regularly. I wasn't close to him for a long time, but he drove down from Tennessee and stayed with my dad in the hospital many nights. Jerry slept right next to Dad in a hospital chair, and so did Jerry's son, Grant, who had recently lost his son. We all needed each other then. And we still do. I am thankful for these relationships strengthening, but I still want my dad back.

Another positive is that I now better understand what others might feel when suffering a loss. And I will never, ever, tell them it happened for a reason.

4) Everything will be OK.

> » No.
> » No. It isn't OK. SOMEONE DIED.
> » What is your definition of OK? Because I think yours is different from mine.
> » My dad died. Is that OK to you? How is that even a little OK? I get that I have to get over it, but it's definitely not OK for me right now.
> » Everything is not ok. None of this is OK.

- This is the only comment that upset me at the time but actually became more true later. Even if someone dies, it will be OK. It may not feel OK. But we have to get used to awful feelings and adjust to carrying loss. Otherwise we just can't go forward. Eventually it is OK, and we do go forward.
- But sometimes the timing of that type of comment is off. EVERYTHING DOES NOT FEEL OK RIGHT NOW. And then you... breathe... I guess.
- I think it is never OK. But you, as a person, are OK. Breathe.

Also, people are going to keep saying things that do not help in a given moment, even when they mean well. And that's... OK.

And we can still want to punch those people in the face sometimes while we are gracious and smile and nod. And feeling that way is OK too.

17

THE CONCENTRIC CIRCLES OF IMPACT

One day I was on the phone with my friend Cior. She sails yachts for a living, and by that I mean she travels all over the world picking up newly purchased vessels, and she works with a team to deliver them to the new owner, often literally an ocean away.

Cior often knows the exact right thing to say. She lost both of her parents at a young age, and she had great advice on dealing with loss.

I mentioned to her how it was surreal to be going through my own grief and have people come up to me at my father's funeral expressing THEIR grief, and I somehow ended up consoling THEM.

Cior mentioned the idea of concentric circles of impact. The people in the middle are going through the most trauma. And then there's one layer out who are still hurting, but they're not hurting like the people in the center. The people in the center lean on the ones in that next layer out. And if that next layer needs to lean on anyone, then they lean outward to the next layer, and so on. You don't lean inward. They are healing themselves.

As an example of this, when my good friend lost her sister, I was sad, but I didn't reach out to that friend to console ME about her sister dying. My friend who lost her sister is the one in the middle. Of course I was there for her, and when I needed to talk about it for myself, I talked about it with others, who were more removed from the situation. They're the outer rings.

I think most people instinctively know to do this, but not everyone, and I thought this was a really great way to frame this idea.

Hug in, lean back.

18

EVERYONE HAS
AN OPINION

I spent several months with my parents, helping with the transition of my dad from being sick to being not with us, and then trying to figure out how my mom at 81 would cope with that and determining how much help she would need. I gave up on any form of a traditional job search in order to help my mom. I did do contract work that allowed me to work remotely.

Two comments were especially offensive to me in this time:

- 1) From a cousin with an accusing tone: "You need to go back to San Francisco. What value are you providing by being with your mom?"

  » Me:

  - Are you kidding me?
  - I just lost a parent. What value is it to keep the other one alive? I am trying to make sure I don't lose Mom too.
  - Is she OK by herself? You can't answer that by spending 30 minutes with her. I've been helping

her every day for months to see where she needs help and where she doesn't.

- Also, maybe *I* need to be home with my mother since my father just died. I'm grieving with her. Maybe SHE is providing value to ME.
- I'm 40 years old. I don't have to justify myself or my choices to you or anyone else, bitch.

- 2) From same cousin: "You need to get a real job."

  » Me:

    - First of all, I did not ask for your opinion on my employment, nor do you know what I'm doing.
    - Second, I have four jobs that let me work remotely. It's called the "gig economy". You maybe wouldn't know about that since you don't work.
    - Third, have you seen how much work it is to do what my dad was doing managing my mom and three dwellings? Well, now I'm doing it.
    - Just for starters: Our dryer now works, our refrigerator works, our house is now painted, our bills are scheduled, the outside light three floors up has been replaced, our garage doors are functional, the garage apartment now has hot water and an electrical grid that doesn't create scary dangerous electrical arcs, and our dishwasher is fixed. I made friends with all of the neighbors (even the ones that Dad cussed out two years ago). I've learned about electrical issues and plumbing. I have a list of Mom's doctors and medication schedules. I've made instruction manuals for how to use the thermostat, the TV, the phone, the computer, and I've labelled everything to make things easier for

my mom. All while working (again, FOUR jobs.) Anyone questioning me can get out of the room and go suck their thumb in a corner if they don't like what I'm doing.

To avoid this person's gaslighting, I began to keep a list of things I was doing in order to justify my time spent with MY OWN MOM. I was running a household and pretending like I wasn't, because my mom wasn't used to her CHILD being in charge. I came into the house at night to do half of those things so she wouldn't know I was doing them.

» So I have a real job. A very real job. Thanks.

In addition to comments about my work situation, people continually had comments about how to handle other things they had no business talking about. A family friend chastised me for sneaking my dad butterscotch slivers in the hospital. Yes, I broke the rules, and he wasn't supposed to have anything to eat, but that was the happiest moment he had in two months, and I'd do it again in a heartbeat.

Never again will I let other people make me feel guilty when I know I'm doing the best thing.

19

THE NEW NORMAL

We ran out of the old normal.

For me, the new normal is an avalanche of emotion, change, and recalibration of responsibilities.

Where am I going to live now? Does Mom need help? Do I need help? Does Mom want to live in California? Do I want to live in Alabama? Which job do I need to be working on today? Where is my cat? Oh, right, he died in the middle of all of this and is in my freezer in San Francisco because I didn't have the time for dealing with that right then.

This doesn't feel like a new normal. This feels like a sneaky nightmare.

Don't worry, the cat isn't still in my freezer. He's buried in Golden Gate Park in San Francisco, which may be a felony, but no one can prove anything.

The new normal is grief at first.

Actually, no. For me it wasn't grief at first, because I had a host of things to take care of which distracted me from grief. Here's a short list of things that needed to be addressed:

Removing Dad's clothes and remnants of being sick, like spit cups and diapers

Making a list of all the bills we had to pay, paying them, and changing them over to my mom's name or mine

Enrolling everything on autopay that I could
    House, medical, and car insurance
    Water, gas, electric, and internet bills
    Social Security deposits for Mom

Converting Mom's prescriptions to automated mail delivery

Paying the property tax bills

Organizing all the paperwork we'll need for taxes next year

Paying for our annual car registrations which were about to expire

Making sure we have the right insurance information in the glove compartment of the car

Putting air in the tires on Mom's car

Getting bank access for me to help with all the transitions

Sending the Power of Attorney paperwork to banks and doctors

Getting the Death Certificate and sending it to institutions who need it

Updating all the titles on the bank accounts that were joint but are now just Mom's

Updating one account that is now joint for Mom and myself so that I can help her

Rolling Dad's retirement accounts over to Mom

Finding someone to mow the lawn

Dealing with the insurance people when a tree fell on the house

Fixing the little red flag on the mailbox, so we could signal outgoing mail

Changing the lightbulbs in the garage

Putting fire extinguishers at the house and in the garage

Putting smoke and carbon monoxide detectors in the house

Setting up a grocery delivery service so I can order things for Mom no matter where I am

Breathe Breathe Breathe

I'm not complaining. I was genuinely thankful to be busy.

As all of this is happening, roles continued to shift, which was uncomfortable. .

Regarding things my father would have normally done, now we have to figure out who does those things. Me, Mom, or we outsource it. And I've been taking on most of it, because my mom is not accustomed to handling things like insurance, investments, and house & car maintenance. I outsourced lawn care immediately, because you're not going to find me on a riding lawn mower yet. Many of the things that need to get done cannot be outsourced. Also, for some of the things my mom used to do, I'm now shifting to doing those as well (laundry, ironing, organizing, cooking, surrepticiously logging into her email in order to clean out her inbox so it's easier for her to use).

Meanwhile, my mother thinks I'm trying to control everything. I know this because she wrote that on a sticky note. Actually, several. There are sticky notes all over the house.

I'm not trying to control everything.

I AM controlling everything.

Someone has to do all of this, and she isn't going to do most of it, or she will get confused and frustrated in trying to, so it's so much easier if I just handle it and let her be mad at me. That is difficult, but that is where we are. The alternative is that she'd be negatively impacted eventually if I don't help her.

In the absence of my help, let's say the house insurance expires and a tree falls on the house again (a very real possibility). Now, we'd have a very expensive problem. Someone who is NOT HER needs to manage things like insurance. That is not something I can get a cousin to do or hire someone to do. I am it. I am the only one. We can't outsource resposibility.

I know she feels like I'm overstepping, but she doesn't see that my intentions are purely to help her. Dad did a lot of work to keep everything going for forty years, and she isn't used to doing it, so she's not going to, and she doesn't know how to. That's fine. I know how.

So I'm being responsible and helping her, but to her that doesn't feel good, so she's often frustrated and angry with me. And I just have to deal with that.

The new normal.

There was also a lot of adjusting to do in being home for several months because Mom and I are living very different lives. Different diets, different sleep schedules, different things we like to do.

There is a business concept that applies here. The concept of Forming, Storming, Norming and Performing (FSNP) describes the four stages of psychological development a team goes through as they work on a project. Teams move through each stage as they overcome challenges, learn to work together and eventually focus on accomplishing a shared goal.

We are in the Storming and grasping at the Norming.

There are some positive changes that came out of Dad not being in charge anymore though.

First, our household no longer buys scratchy single-ply toilet paper from the dollar store.

Also, Dad used to insist on all the appliances being turned off during thunderstorms. He would literally yell at us if we didn't turn things off, including the air conditioner. There are a lot of thunderstorms in Alabama in the summer, so there was more yelling in the summer. After Dad died, I checked with all the neighbors, and no one else does this. It took me a while to unbrainwash my mom on this.

And Mom now leaves the doors open for the cat, even with the air conditioner on, because she doesn't want to have to get up every time the cat wants to be on the other side of the door, which could be in 20 second increments.

Also, Mom now gets to keep the house at the temperature she wants without my dad yelling at her about wasting energy. She's 81 years old. She's cold. Go ahead and turn that heat up, Mom.

Also, that brand new car she wanted, which I'll explain later, Dad would have never in a million years let that happen. Again, she's 81 years old, and she finally has a car that she feels proud to drive. I'm not judging her for that feeling because when I visit her, I'm now the one driving her old minivan, and I hate that thing too. When you drive it over a rock too hard the rear plastic bumper panel pops off. She's been driving a trash car for ten years.

I started keeping a list of things I could do with her. She likes *Wheel of Fortune* and any Hallmark movie since they all have happy endings. But my favorite new form of entertainment was the possum. I'll explain.

My parents didn't like to let anything go to waste, so whenever someone didn't finish a sandwich or if the cats didn't eat all of their food, the remainder went into the possum bowl. The smell of the bowl was nauseating, but I liked the possum, so I fully supported this possum bowl idea.

Every night we placed the possum bowl out in the yard about ten feet from the house, and we left an outside light on so we could see any activity in the yard. Around eight p.m., the possum would come waddling up. He was fairly punctual. It was always a happy moment when we saw him. One of us would whisper excitedly, "The possum is here!" This started well before my dad got sick. And I was happy to have something fun to share with my mom at her house every night once dad was gone.

The possum bowl. Part of my new normal.

20

GRIEF

OK, so things like insurance and lightbulbs got handled. Is it time to grieve yet? I don't know. When do you grieve? What is grief?

People sometimes say there are five stages of grief. I beg to differ. I don't know how many stages it is, but it feels more like five thousand to me. It's not linear, and I'm not sure it ever goes away. I've heard that you just learn to feel hurt and sit with it.

I am not there yet, but I'm trying.

I started a new contract job a few months after Dad died, and one morning before work, one of my dad's friends called me to ask if there was a good number to reach him because he wasn't answering his phone.

No. There's not a good number for him.

Most of the time I could talk about what happened matter of factly, but this day I couldn't. Through tears, I told his friend what happened.

I went to work after that call. My friend at work cheerfully greeted me and asked me how I was, and I burst into tears again. My whole work team was so kind and understanding.

Another friend said, sometimes you're just going to have a "bad dad day". People will understand.

Yes, the good people will understand.

Others have said things like "Why are you still sad? Didn't he die months ago?" As if I'm just supposed to be over it after 6 months.

I'm sorry to inconvenience you with my being sad about my dad dying. What is your acceptable timeline for feeling bad about that? Do I get to feel better after 30 days or is it 90?

Or IS IT NEVER?

I don't know.

But I am sure I can't control it.

I'm not TRYING to be sad. It just happens. And it can come at inconvenient times.

Having lost someone I deeply love makes me compassionate about the changing waves of grief in others.

Here are the official five stages of grief: Denial, Anger, Bargaining, Depression and Acceptance.

I think these don't come in order and they don't come just once. I've felt acceptance, but then I've still screamed in visceral agony. I've felt anger about things that I can't do anything about.

I also think whoever came up with this list of stages skipped a few. I would add Reconnection and Joyful Memory. Maybe those are part of Acceptance.

58

For me, sadness and joy come in flashes sometimes.

I took the trash out and looked up at the sky and saw the constellation Orion. My dad taught me about constellations when I was little and sitting in his lap at the beach. Just looking at the stars now reminds me of him. I was happy for having that memory, but I cried one time while taking out the trash and seeing the stars, which is, I guess, part of the new normal for me. You don't get to pick when the flashes hit you. But that moment was both joy and sadness.

Now I don't cry when I see Orion, but I do say "Hi, Dad".

And then there are the dreams.

Sometimes Dad is in my dreams. And then I wake up and happily think "I need to call Dad since it's been a while.", and then I remember that I can't. I've cried at those times too.

I think being strong includes being OK with crying. Only weak people think that crying makes you weak.

Sometimes my crying makes people uncomfortable. I've gotten to where I can just have a conversation and cry and say, "Oh, I do this all the time. I'm OK. This is just how I am now."

Some people say "Oh, don't cry". Others say "It's OK to cry". It doesn't really matter what they say. I'm going to cry anyway.

More good advice from friends: Mourn in it, but don't drown in it.

It's really easy to just sink and give up sometimes in grief. I tell myself, swim up when you can.

Another part of the new normal is that I sometimes now think and speak of my father in the present tense. I'll say things like, "Dad likes the car parked like this." Or "Dad likes ice cream too."

I catch myself. It's sort of like when you keep writing the date with the past year when it's January in the new year. It takes a while to adjust.

It's hard to adjust in many ways like that at once. I like to think of him as present tense anyway. He is present in many ways.

21

EVERYONE GRIEVES DIFFERENTLY

My main concern now was how my mom was going to handle life after losing her husband of over 40 years. She seemed mostly alright.

I was depressed, I didn't sleep enough, and I didn't brush my hair unless I had to. I worked in the yard, I painted the basement floor and Dad's workshop. I think I had paint in my hair for a week, and I didn't care. I didn't want to see anyone anyway.

I also washed everything in the house, and then ironed it, including washcloths and underwear. I was really just trying to stay busy.

It also kept me from throwing up constantly, which tended to happen when I had time to think about my dad.

But then I also wanted to think about him. And when I could handle it, I did. You really get to know someone all over again as you go through all of their things. I cleaned out his closet, his bathroom, his desk drawers in the office, all of his files, his books, his bank records, his food. I found notes about investing, about maintenance that the house and the cars needed, reflections on his life, and reflections about MY life, some of which were sweet and some hurtful. I shared a lot of things with my Dad that I didn't tell other people.

A year ago, I'd been pregnant and lost the baby. He thought my life was off track because I wasn't married.

In the same drawer of papers, I found an old flyer from my elementary school days about how to be a good parent. He certainly was that.

I also found a small index card in his wallet. I know what this is. When I was getting divorced ten years ago he asked me how I was handling it, and I said I was OK, but I sometimes had mixed emotions, even though I knew divorce was the right thing to do. He told me to write down the thoughts I wanted to keep, put them on an index card, carry it with me, and just re-read it over and over until those thoughts were the ones that stuck with me.

I'm sure this is what was in his wallet. His notes to himself.

His card was worn, and it started off with the cryptic, "No P" at the top.

Well now we have a mystery to solve. What was "No P"?

I called his brother Jerry and sent him a picture of the card to see if he had any idea what that meant. We both paused to think. Jerry said he didn't want to say what he thought, so I just said it for him, "You don't think it's porn?" And we laughed. Honestly I wouldn't have cared if Dad was into that, but I'm pretty sure he wasn't since I've now gone through every item in the house that was his, and I've used his computer, and absolutely nothing even hinted at that. So we kept brainstorming. This was part of the grief: Connecting with Uncle Jerry and trying to figure out Dad, even now.

After a few days, Uncle Jerry cracked the code. P was about Politics. Jerry said Dad used to go on rants with him about political things. Dad didn't like the new mayor in our city and was counting down the days until the next election. Once we looked at the other notes on the card, it was clear that that's what it was about.

I saved the notecard. It's nice to see his handwriting.

I paid more attention to things he chose to have. I didn't realize he liked birds so much, but now I make sure we have bird seed in the feeder on his office porch. Now I remember him getting excited about blue jays and robins when I was younger. I wish I'd gotten excited too to share his love of birds. I do now.

When I work in his office now, I often leave the door open so I can hear the birds and see them come to the bird feeder. He loved animals. He also liked people.

In going through his desk at the office, I found a notecard in the center of the front drawer. He had written jokes on it. I'd never gone through all of his things before, but I am fairly sure that keeping jokes on hand was a regular practice. He always had new jokes at the ready for the next phone call with a friend.

After he died, there were 41 unplayed messages on his phone at the office. One day after his service, I finally sat down and listened to them. Most of them were from people far away who hadn't heard of his passing. I called every one of them that I could.

Sometimes the phone in the office rang, and for a fraction of a second, I hoped it was him. I knew it wasn't him, but I so wanted it to be him. Months later, I finally unplugged it. It was never going to be him.

In the office, we removed the huge heavy desks, and I bought a small desk and a bed, so I started staying in the office. It's just across the driveway, which is frankly the perfect amount of space between my mom and me.

Part of my grief is about her. I am now sure that my dad was covering for her dementia for years.

I'm glad he passed first, because he loved my mom so much. It would have hurt him to watch her decline. I am honestly thankful that I can be the one to help her instead of him.

22

IS MOM OK ALONE?

The insurance on the cars lasts until September, and then we have to change the name on the policy. We also need to get someone to fix the continually dripping sink in the kitchen. Two trees are well positioned to fall on the house in the next big storm, so we need to cut those down soon. And someone needs to clean out the gutters at some point or we'll end up with roof problems again.

I know Mom won't take care of any of this. And that is just a short list of logistics on managing the house.

Mom is also physically not ok alone. She fell in the yard and didn't tell anyone for a week. It looked like a truck hit her when we saw the bruising. My cousin Dotsy saw it and took her to the hospital. She told the doctor that the fall knocked her unconscious. I was in San Francisco then. We are rolling the dice when she's alone.

She probably needs someone to check on her when I'm not there, but she won't agree to having any help like that. That's the reason I stay with her a lot. She won't let anyone else "help". And she doesn't think of me as helping much either. She still thinks I'm basically on vacation when I'm there. I think we have radically different expectations of what a vacation entails.

Another wrinkle: She often doesn't think I'm even capable of helping her since I'm her child and a female, and to her, females cannot do as much as men can do. A generational bias. I have to get neighbor Don Holley to weigh in on things as small as where to put a plant in the yard.

Handling money is another area where she trusts the opinion of men over me. I was a registered stock broker with Merrill Lynch, I have two masters degrees in finance, and I've worked at five different reputable banks. I'm sure I can handle financial issues just fine. I reminded her of this, and she seemed like she vaguely remembered my credentials in this field and then immediately went back to thinking of me as a child. Great. I have to call a man to get anything done.

She also accuses me of stealing things like her forks and towels. And she accuses me of doing other things that I didn't do. It's not her fault. She's just confused. But her paranoia about many things started percolating well before my dad got sick, so I'm sure it's not just stress from losing him.

23

ROTATE

I started doing all the laundry at Mom's house. I actually like doing laundry, so that worked out well.

One laundry-related conversation especially made me smile. One day I asked Mom if she wanted me to change the sheets on her bed. And she said, "No, they're fine. I just rotate them."

Me: What?

Mom: Yeah, I sleep on one side, and then after a while, I just rotate them.

Me in my head: I'm not sure if this is very redneck or kind of brilliant.

I mean... it's not a terrible idea, but... just wash the sheets!

She's adapting to my being back home more, and I'm adapting to things she's probably been doing for years.

So, fine. We'll rotate the sheets.

24

CLAWS AND FLAWS

Being in a grief-stricken situation brings out the best and worst in people.

I've learned to let some people go.

I've also learned how to be more kind and very forgiving.

I'm going to back up the timeline a little here. One morning while my dad was upstairs dying, (the day before the rabbit died) I was up at five a.m. typing in the kitchen. My mom came down and cooked an egg, and then was really mad at me because a particular spice was gone. I had no idea what she was talking about.

Me: What is the spice that you need?

Mom [angry]: It was something lemon.

Me: OK. I will go get something lemon at the store.

Mom [frustrated]: They don't make it anymore.

Me: OK, well, I need to get prescriptions for you and Dad, and as long as I'm at Walmart anyway, I'll just get all the lemon spices, and we'll see if those are close to what you want.

Mom: [Walks away, still mad at me.]

We were both tired, and it was a very trying time, so I don't blame Mom at all for feeling upset, but I was also frustrated because she was mad at me even while I was trying to help her.

So I go to Walmart at... whatever time Walmart opens. One of my good friends called me as I was parking. And I just needed to vent.

- Me to Friend: DAD is DYING upstairs and Mom is mad at me about fucking spices.
- Friend: You have to stop cursing, Natalie.... I've chosen a different lifestyle than you have.
- Me: [In my head]: Are you fucking serious? Right now? You want to criticize me for words? And my "lifestyle"? Well, my lifestyle is that I left my entire life in California to help my family in Alabama for months and gave up several job offers. I just needed a minute to express that I'm frustrated and upset with THE FACT THAT MY DAD IS DYING - did you get that part? - and my mom is focused on spices. And you're worried that I'm using a couple of curse words in expressing frustration.
- Me: [out loud]: Speachless.
- Friend: You wouldn't say those words if I were Muslim.
- Me: ...What?? YES I FUCKING WOULD, BECAUSE ANY ACTUAL FRIEND WOULD KNOW THAT I SPEAK LIKE THIS WHEN..... I NEED TO. What does being Muslim have anything to do with this conversation? It's kind of a bad time to impose your new vocabulary morals on me. Thank you for letting me know about YOUR needs though. I think we shouldn't talk right now.

I lost all respect for her in that moment. We haven't talked since. Lifestyle, my ass.

I understand that frequent cursing is unbecoming to some people, but there is no reason to impose a moral high ground about it when someone is under exceptional stress.

On nurse Mabel's first day with my dad, she told him that her husband had passed years ago, and he had been a preacher. Dad apologized in advance, and said to her, "Sometimes I cuss."

Without hesitation, Mabel said, "That's OK. For all we know, Jesus cussed too. We don't know what he said in the temple when he flipped over those tables."

Dad didn't really curse that much, but it was sweet that Mabel was so nice about his warning.

I don't curse very often either, but the spices day was not a normal day. To me, in that moment, friendship meant listening to me rant for two minutes about "the fucking spices". Thankfully, other friends were there to listen, and we still laugh about it now. If a friend comes up behind me and whispers, "fucking spices", I start laughing.

So after that ridiculous conversation, I got out of the car, got the prescriptions we needed, and I bought all the versions of lemon spices carried by our neighborhood store.

Ruling out a friend who wasn't helpful in my time of need was necessary. She was sapping my energy with arguing, and I just didn't have the energy to give.

I didn't want to rule out a mom though. And this is when I started to learn how to better help her. That learning curve wasn't pretty.

I lost my temper with Mom one day. I hadn't slept. I was packing to fly out later that day, and the very first thing she said to me that morning when I greeted her was, "When you're back in California, I'm not buying your groceries."

Me: What?

She had not been buying my groceries anyway, and I never asked her to. I bought HER groceries. And I was going through MY savings to be with her and Dad.

I told her that I didn't expect her to pay for anything for me, but after six months of helping Dad and her and not earning my normal salary, it hurt my feelings that groceries would be something that would even be a thought or concern. And we haven't even considered the long-term impact on my career, given that she is going to need substantial help now that Dad is gone.

She said "Well, this is your choice." And "This is just what children do."

No. No, it's not.

Some children are incapable of helping, logistically, emotionally, financially.

I had saved enough to give myself time to help for a while. I don't have kids, so I was flexible enough to stay when it really mattered.

So, yes, it's a choice, but NOT everyone does it. And I wanted to scream "It is absolutely NOT just what children do. It's what YOUR child is doing!"

I was so frustrated in that moment, because there was such a lack of recognition of what I gave to our family.

And was there actually a choice? When did I really have a choice to leave?

When she was running a fever, fell in the bathtub, and I picked her up and carried her to the bed? When we went to the emergency room in the middle of the night and I was running upstairs to check on Dad in the ICU and downstairs to check on Mom in the ER? When Dad was unconscious? Maybe when we had to wipe feces off of him and change the diaper the day the helpers didn't come? How about the day of the funeral? Would THAT have been a great day to leave? No. I would never leave under any of those circumstances. It's technically a choice to stay, but to me it really didn't feel like a choice. I was staying there to help and to get things done. And I did. I am genuinely thankful to be able to help. Also, you're fucking welcome.

I did not say any of that out loud.

"Well you're staying here for free."

"NO. I WORK here for free."

I didn't want to yell at her, so I walked outside and roar-screamed. I cracked instead of bending.

It scared her. And I felt so bad for scaring her. That was also the day I recognized that I wasn't dealing with a logical person, and it is going to be a completely thankless job to help her, possibly for years, so I HAD to get a grip on how to work with her without getting upset myself.

I spent the next two days watching videos on how to help dementia patients. It helped me to understand what my mom is going through, and how to help her without taking some of her more hurtful comments personally. It also set my expectations for what was ahead.

Fucking spices.

25

ANGER

I'm angry at myself for not helping my dad more.

I'm angry that the cardiac surgeon called Dad a risky patient and wouldn't operate to try to fix his heart, because it would throw off the surgeon's success metrics if Dad died.

I'm angry that the hospital sent him home without a lung drain. They could have helped him live longer.

I'm angry that the newspaper keeps being delivered after I asked them to stop.

I'm angry that it's so hot in Alabama in July.

None of these are actually things to be angry about, because being angry doesn't help anything. But that didn't stop me from being angry.

My anger came from feeling helpless.

26

SHIFTING PRIORITIES

Mom.

What are we dealing with now? Does Mom want to live alone? Can she?

Yes, she wants to live at her home of 40-plus years, with her two cats.

One cat is sweet and hilariously dives spread eagle onto the kitchen counter while knocking everything off. The other is a svelte black petite chipmunk assassin. If there is a cat mafia, she rules it.

I want Mom to stay at home if she can. It's a big house for one person, and there are a lot of potential risks like stairs and uneven rocks outside, so that worries me, but she and I talked about maybe moving to a nice retirement place one day, and she's not ready yet. I do think she'd like the social aspect of being in a retirement community, but I am definitely not going to try to force her to go. She'd just call a cab and come right back home anyway. Also, if it were me, I wouldn't want to go either. I'd wait until I had to, and so that's what we agreed on.

I am anticipating that she will eventually fall again and one day badly hurt herself.

Our family has done a lot of things intended to keep my mom safe. Installing railings in the bathtub, adding LED lights on the stairway bannister, etc... And those things will help.

But none of that will save her from losing brain functioning.

Dementia is brain failure, not just memory problems. So it eventually impacts motor skills as well as judgement.

As this escalates, there is a tradeoff in maintaining safety versus maintaining control and dignity.

When do you take the car keys away? Or the checkbook?

I do not know the answers to those questions, but I do know I need to stay with her as much as I can. Her brain is unraveling slowly.

My life feels like it is unraveling slowly too. My career, my body, my boyfriend, my friendships. But I'm trying to hold that San Francisco rope while building a new rope in Birmingham by developing my friendships, reaching out to neighbors, seeing family, and connecting with the community by volunteering.

27

TRADEOFFS

When you're doing everything in your power to help someone else, it's hard to take care of yourself.

I didn't eat much, but somehow I gained about 20 pounds in a year. I threw my scale out, so I'm not sure of any exact amounts on weight change, but my physique certainly shifted and I lost a lot of muscle tone and strength.

Prior to flying home to Alabama, I went to the gym almost every day to lift weights, and I loved it, but the stress of taking care of my parents derailed me psychologically. Being in Alabama for so long took me out of my routine, and I stopped going to the gym.

Aside from not going to the gym, I was doing the best I could mentally. I called my therapist a few times. I also called friends and family that were supportive. That helped.

In normal times, taking care of myself is doing meaningful work, working out, learning, traveling, eating properly, finding a creative outlet, talking with friends, and taking warm baths.

Life still includes most of those things.

And so now, does taking care of myself mean that I go back to San Francisco and pursue an office job? That isn't possible. I cannot take phone calls from Mom with questions like, "Where is my blue shirt?" when I have a regular job with meetings all day. For now, that option is just out. Taking care of myself means letting go of feeling bad about the tradeoffs I'm making.

It's Mom versus career right now. I can always get another great job. I can't always get another great Mom. She took care of me for my first years. I can take care of her in her last years. That seems fair.

Another trade off is that I do want to explore the world, but I also don't want to leave my mom alone. If I left, it wouldn't be far. There were many reasons not to travel. I've already spent the better part of a year blowing through my savings to stay with Dad and her. I resent that she can't see that, and I also feel bad that I resent it, because it's not her fault that she can't be logical enough to see it.

This phase of care is a careful dance of seeing how close is too close and how far is too far. Living in the house with her is way too close. I cannot get any work done if I'm staying at the house, because my mom frequently talks to me, herself, or the cats, and I listen to all of it in case she's saying something that requires attention. So I can't focus on work if I'm in the house with her.

Staying in the garage apartment across the driveway is a great alternative. I'm close enough to help, but we're not right on top of each other. She can live her new normal. And I can live... my life of limbo. In between jobs, in between cities, in between boyfriends...

28

MAKING FRIENDS

When my dad was in the hospital, I often stayed to talk with him until he fell asleep. One night that conversation ended about two a.m. It was a good conversation, but heavy. When my car came to pick me up I collapsed in the back seat. I was emotionally exhausted and asked if there was a place to grab a drink at that hour. The driver took me to Marty's, an after hours bar close to the hospital. They stay open until six a.m. Perfect. My hours are all off anyway. That's where I encountered a frozen wine machine and a red-haired 6'6' gentleman named Josh. He is one of the nicest people I've ever met. He worked long hours in the service industry, so he was often up as late as I was.

After my dad died, I fully renovated the office/garage apartment. Sometimes I was up at two a.m. putting together Ikea-caliber furniture, and Josh offered to come over and help me after his shifts ended. He also helped me write directions for operating Mom's TV and DVD player in the middle of the night. He helped me with many things around the house late at night. We would normally crash around four or five a.m. I'd be back up around seven or eight a.m. and let him sleep while I worked.

I usually asked Josh to park around the corner so my mom wouldn't see his car. I didn't want her to come over asking questions.

I'm over 40 years old. I really don't need to worry about what anyone thinks about my actions or perceived actions. However, to my mom, I'm a child. This is how dementia works.

The reality is, we're adults, and it's no one's business what we were doing. But usually we were putting furniture together and then falling asleep.

Whatever we were doing, it was part of taking care of myself. After six months of being in Alabama, I now had one single male friend, and he didn't mind that I liked staying up until five a.m. fixing things and doing chores.

Yet I felt guilty spending time with him like that, because I didn't want Mom to feel uncomfortable. And I know she would if she thought I were sleeping next to someone I'm not married to. Literally just sleeping next to a man would not be OK for her.

I didn't want to disturb my mother's sense of propriety if I could help it, but eventually I just decided… maybe she won't notice or care or remember. Also, she is already upset at me for stealing things, which I'm not doing. If she's going to be mad anyway, I should just do what makes me happy. Having a friend come over and spend time with me makes me happy.

If I were in San Francisco all the time, I'd have my San Francisco boyfriend staying over (hypothetical boyfriend), and Mom wouldn't see that. But now that I'm much closer, she sees more of my life. I know what it looks like if someone stays with me all night, but no one knows what happens behind closed doors. Sometimes people are lonely and just need to be hugged all night or to just sleep next to someone. I like having another person near me. And that is part of taking care of myself.

29

THERAPY

Seeing the process of Dad dying was hard, but at least he was lucid and logical until the end. We had real conversations, and by that I mean, they were important, well thought-out. We talked about everything from financial logistics to relationships. And he recognized what I was sacrificing in order to be with him and Mom. I was giving up relationships and job opportunities.

My mom just didn't see it the same way he did. She thought I was just on vacation to be there, and that absolutely broke my heart, because it was clear that she thought I was taking, when I was truly, honestly giving everything I had. Unlike Dad, she did not have compassion for me, because she didn't know. It isn't her fault. But it was painful to not be able to sit down and make a plan for both of us that made sense.

She isn't logical, and she isn't my mom anymore. She is a person that I care about and love. The original person is gone, and now I have a new person to love and take care of. She thinks I steal things from the house, and she's mad at me often.

That's when I went to therapy. I am doing my absolute best, and… my mom is still upset with me.

So the expectations here are:
>Stay and help her (That's just what children do.)
>Get a regular job
>Assume all the responsibilities Dad had managed
>Handle the new responsibilities that arise in his absence
>Figure out how to manage someone with dementia
>Take care of myself

My therapist said to me, "You can't live up to the standards of some-one who isn't using logic."

True.

But it still feels bad to be judged by a parent, even if the one judging is imposing unreasonable expectations.

I don't have thick skin. It's part of my charm. I have strong compassion, which is what makes it so hard when my mom is upset. The other end of the spectrum is just not caring how she is or how she feels. And if that were my attitude, I'd just go right back to my San Francisco life and let Mom fend for herself.

That's just not something I can do. I want to be with her now, even if it doesn't feel great. It does feel right.

30

FEELING CORNERED

I hate this.

Dad is dead. Mom is accusing me of stealing things when she can't remember where she put them, which ironically means she might need me to stay with her MORE. Anyone near the house is fair game for being blamed for stealing including workers, neighbors, family – but mostly me.

I want to work, and during all of this I have job interviews with great companies, but I can't leave my mom. And when I say leave, I mean that even if I leave Birmingham, I don't feel like I can be unavailable, ever.

If she falls, I need to be able to take that call and help her. Even if I'm 3000 miles away, I can send help. At minimum, I have to be available.

Several people have suggested that I get her one of the "I've fallen and I can't get up" necklaces.

Sure. Those work. If you wear them. Which I know she will not. I can't even get her to charge her cell phone. Anything technology-related that's new is just not happening. And also, she's not wearing something tacky like that. (I wouldn't either. They really ought to make cuter ones.) But she can use the phone, and I know she'd call me if she fell and could reach a phone. I bought extra phones to make sure they are very accessible all over the house.

When she calls me now, I never know if she's fallen, or she's just saying hi, or if she thinks someone broke into the house and stole a piece of paper that "disappeared".

I am always on high alert.

Even when I take naps, I often sleep with my phone on my chest in case she calls.

I just can't imagine having a normal job now unless they are exceptionally understanding.

Perhaps this is like parents who feel the pull to stay at home when they have a baby, and they prioritize that over their career.

Right now, this feels like having a child with a Lexus and a checkbook.

I know she isn't a child. She is an adult, and I respect her and her wishes.

I want to have a normal job, but I also want to have a mom. I want to be there for her. My most important "job" now is to protect and care for her, even if she doesn't see what I'm doing. That's more important to me than any other job I've ever had.

I talked about these kinds of things with friends and family that I thought would compassionately listen, because that helped me to feel better. Most people kindly listened and understood. And then my cousin told me I was acting like a martyr.

So let me get this straight. I can't share how I'm feeling without my own cousin judging me and calling me names?

Get out. Really, leave. What a useless and ignorant insult.

I certainly spoke with a lot of people in our family a lot, and maybe it sounded like I was trying to get sympathy, but I really just needed someone to talk to. Everyone else was kind to me when I needed to vent.

People who haven't been long term caretakers sometimes do not understand.

31

WHO IS MOM?

I love my mom. I love her as the person who was the mom that I knew for most of my life, and now I love her as whoever she is becoming. She is not the mom I know anymore.

Mom getting upset about the spices was the first big red flag. Getting upset about Dad's brother Jerry "stealing" her blue shirt was the next one. Again, I wrote that off as stress in the moment, but six months after Dad's passing, on Christmas morning I greeted Mom, and she was upset that someone had stolen the bow off of the garage door. She was really upset and was sure some kids did it.

What had actually happened was that the garage door was up instead of down. I had raised it, so that I could drive somewhere. So the bow was still on the door but not visible. I suggested that we go out and see if we could find the bow by pulling the door back down. So we went to look, and of course the bow was there. She was relieved. But handling that felt like talking with a child who doesn't have object permanence.

Also, it's a bow. No one goes around stealing Christmas bows. We are losing logic.

One of the more frequent topics of conversation with her now is that things are "disappearing".

Mom is having trouble remembering how to do things like use the thermostat and the TV, so I've written step-by-step instructions for her. I have no idea where she's putting these instructions. She doesn't either. She thinks someone has come into the house and stolen the instructions.

Her paranoia is part of what is happening to her. I cannot use logic anymore with these situations.

No one breaks into the house and steals instructions for how to use a TV and then doesn't take the TV.

She also thinks I am taking things from her. She definitely thinks I stole her checkbook, ipad, and car keys. I did none of those things. I am only trying to help her.

And very often she cannot remember the words for things, so she ends up describing them. Like when she couldn't remember the word for "wall', she tried describing it as "like the floor but this way" [gesturing up and down].

This was really distressing for me at first.

"It's the disease." This is what a close family friend keeps telling me when things like this happen.

We still had fun though, too. We went out for lunch every week or so. My boyfriend Ken worked at the hospital down the street from one of our favorite spots, so he met us often. On one of those days, Mom said she needed to pack up and go see Mother. Her mother died about 30 years ago.

I didn't want to upset her, so I just said "Your mother isn't home right now". After a few moments, she asked, "Is she dead?" And I said "Yes". She said she wished she'd been there. I assured her that she had been there and that she was a wonderful daughter, and her mom had the best doctors and the nicest room at the hospital with gorgeous views of Birmingham, and we had a great birthday party for her there. All of that was true.

Mom: "Is Daddy dead too?"

Me: [With tears streaming down my face] "Yes"

So I'm silently crying at the restaurant, feeling empathy because she's learning that her parents are gone. And then we got in the car, and she didn't say anything else about it. She was fine. I think she'd already forgotten the whole conversation by then.

Several people in my family have suggested that I make her go to a retirement community for her safety.

Cousin: "Would you let a five year old stay in a house alone?"

Of course not, but she's not a five-year-old. She's in her eighties and has lucid moments and less lucid moments. She's generally just fine. She just forgets things sometimes, as we all do. We are venturing into uncharted territories here.

My focus now is: What can I do to bring her joy?

Answer: Keep her at home with her cats and her TV. And bring her chocolate pie sometimes.

I asked her if she wanted to travel anywhere, because I thought maybe we only had a little time left to do it again.

She said no.

She wants to keep everything the same. Change is bad. Traveling would not be fun for her right now.

My mom is not clinically diagnosed with dementia, but the signs are there. I'm not sure how we'd get a diagnosis, since she won't go to the neurologist to take the tests for it. We set up the appointment several times, but she keeps moving it when they call to remind her, and when I ask her about that, it's clear that she just doesn't want to go.

I know she's having memory and brain failure, so what would it help to get tested? I already know what the results would be. I also already have Power of Attorney for her in case I need to help her with legal and medical things.

I wish there were a way to have Power of Emotion.

And I wish there were a way to have my mom back.

32

LEARNING

I can't control Mom's emotions, but I can control mine. And I can educate myself on how to help her. I've now studied how to help. These are my main notes. If you're going through something similar with someone you love, maybe they will help.

First, BREATHE. Apparently caretakers forget to do this.

Others' behavior follows ours. Show up calm and happy. They will likely reflect that back.

How I feel is real and important, and how Mom feels is real and important.

She cannot help what is happening. None of these changes are from her not trying.

I know she is doing the best she can.

Also, in trying to help, don't force it. If Mom doesn't want help with something, just let her be.

Dementia is not only memory problems. It is brain failure. It is an umbrella term that includes Alzheimers, the most common form of dementia.

You lose your words first. That's the left side of the brain.

The right side is retained better. It responds more to music, poetry, dancing, and prayer. And cursing. Ha!

Apparently there's often a phase where there's cursing and sex talk. We have not gotten there yet. But that might be entertaining.

The meaning of words becomes less understandable, but emotion and rhythm of words comes through. So if I were to get angry with her, the thought on her end could be "I get that you're mad at me, but I don't know why." And that could be scary for her.

Hearing that that's how Mom might feel, and maybe already has, completely broke my heart. I will try to never make her feel like I'm mad at her. I love her so much. I have always tried to be patient and loving with her, but now I know I really have to try extra hard. I'm never mad at her anymore. I'm sad at her.

I love this person, whoever she is and whoever she evolves to be.

Advice from a family friend who experienced this with his mother: Remember, it's a disease, not her. When she's confused, go along with it. Don't use logic. It won't work. It's not there. Tactics: remove things from sight, change the subject, agree and procrastinate. Things will go missing. Let it go. When she says things about people stealing or moving things or things disappearing, say things like, "I'm sorry that happened."

Because to her, it happened.

33

BLAME

Constantly being blamed for stealing things hurts. It feels unjust. You want to defend yourself and explain, and to some degree I tried to, but experts say it's best not to argue with someone with dementia.

One of the most repeated accusations from Mom was that I stole her iPad.

She asked me for help with getting her email working, so I did pick up her iPad, but I didn't take it, and I didn't actually change anything. Her email was working just fine. I think she just forgot that you have to click on the blue mail envelope to get to it. So I tried to show her how to do that, but she didn't want to hear it because she insisted that was not her iPad; I'd taken hers. I showed her that we can tell that it's hers because it has the labels I made for her with her name and phone number on it in case it was lost in the hospital. She got really mad and said "Well that one is red, and mine is pink. Dad's was red. You have mine somewhere."

This confusion is understandable. Years ago, my dad did have a red one, and my mom did have a pink one. However, those covers she's thinking of were really worn out, so two years ago for Christmas I got new covers for their iPads. I reminded my mom about that, and she angrily said "I would never choose RED. Mine is PINK!"

She was wrong. She chose red two years ago. She just doesn't remember. I didn't argue though. I just said, "It's OK. We'll change it." And I took off the red cover and ordered a pink one.

It is easier to blame me than to consider that she's losing her memory, and I don't want to make her feel bad.

When I changed it to pink: "That's better but it's not the same pink."

She's right about that. It's not the same pink, but... her iPad is old and they don't make that pink anymore, and I tried.

Someone gave me advice about this kind of circumstance. When you can't defend yourself, it takes a lot of energy. Over time, it feels like abuse, and like you're not allowed to escape. It's bad for your mental health. You have to have a way to escape.

That was true.

I needed to get away from this. So I drove up to Dad's cabin. I needed to check on some things up there anyway.

Dad built a cabin in the woods in the middle of nowhere about two hours from our house. It's nearly impossible to find, and it's become my refuge where I can get my own work done and be close to my mom if she needs me. And I don't get accused of stealing things, since I'm not near the house. Well, usually I'm not accused of stealing things.

Once, I was on my way there, and I got a call from our bank manager while I was driving. It was mom accusing me of stealing her checkbook because she couldn't find it, and clearly I'd taken it and run off.

She wanted to cancel all the remaining checks in the checkbook and to let me know she was mad at me. "I'm tired of you doing all of this stuff, and I'm just SICK OF IT!"

Right. Great.

The branch manager at the bank knows the situation, and he knows me. I spoke with him and assured him I didn't have the checkbook, and I said they are welcome to cancel the checks, but she'll eventually find them wherever she hid them and then use them, and then they'll start bouncing, so it would be better to just order new checks for her and leave the old ones still valid. I later found the checkbook in a drawer, but I didn't tell her, because I know she'd suspect me of planting it or snooping (When I found the checkbook, I was helping her look for her car keys which she also thought I'd taken.)

The checkbook beratement further incented me to stay at the cabin longer. Every time she loses something, it's my fault, and there is absolutely nothing I can do to lessen the frequency of accusations except to be somewhere else.

34

ESCAPE

The cabin is small and simple, but it's just perfect to me. One bedroom downstairs, a loft upstairs with two twin beds, a small bathroom, a fireplace, a couch, a small kitchen, and a dining table. It's on ten wooded acres, and the house overlooks a beautiful valley. A train comes through the valley every hour or so, and I can faintly hear the whistle blowing. The sunsets are a gorgeous mix of orange, pink, and yellow. When the breeze comes, the trees rustle. And when bad weather comes, the thunderstorms are powerful. Around June, it's magical to stand in the dark forest and watch the fireflies.

When Dad died, at first I thought we should sell the cabin because Mom didn't care about going there, and it didn't seem practical for me to visit it much. But I needed an electrician to come out and fix some things, so I ended up spending a couple of weeks there for that. And after being there, I can see how much of Dad is in that house. He designed every part of it with his mind, and he built it with his hands.

When I walk in, I now think, "Hi Dad." When you see someone else's artwork, you get to know them a little better. He would never call himself an artist, but that place was truly his art.

I will never let it go.

Being there is one of my ways of taking care of myself.

I work on my computer while I'm there, but when I take breaks, I like all the opportunities for manual labor. I built a large fire pit, I started moving rocks as a trim around the driveway, I like to rake leaves around the house, and I learned to use the weedeater. Sparks flew when I used a hatchet to break an old chain off the front gate.

I also got rid of everything in the cabin that looked like it was from a garage sale.

Aside from the train rolling through the valley and the occasional rustle of leaves and animals, it's quiet.

I don't mind solitude. Except I'm not totally alone there.

Eagles, hedgehogs, and hawks keep me company in the daytime. At night the raccoons come.

I threw out some food one day (we don't have trash service out there, so everything that decomposes just goes in the woods), and that night I saw the raccoons having a party with my leftovers. This is the only entertainment I have besides my laptop, so I bought dog treats and left one on the window sill in front of the dining table where I work. The first night of this, while I was typing, a little paw slowly came up over the top of the dog treat and grabbed it. It made me laugh. So I kept putting treats out. I initiated a lot of raccoon parties.

The racoons came as long as I didn't have Athena with me. Athena is the neighbor's dog. I've made friends with the neighbors, which has been an adventure unto itself.

I'd talked on the phone with neighbor Martha. My dad was a friend of Martha's husband, Griff, who passed a few years ago. I reached out to Martha to let her know about my dad. It turned out that her son Jeff lives in the house next to me. We can faintly see each other's houses through the woods.

Martha has a huge heart. When she sees an animal or a person in need, she does everything she can to make things better. She even moves roadkill out of the road, because she doesn't want it to be run over again.

Martha worked with law enforcement as a juvenile officer for years. When one woman gave birth and couldn't take care of the baby, Martha adopted this baby boy who needed help. And that's how she adopted Alexander. She homeschools him, and they take care of dogs, cats, chickens, roosters, and an arthritic cow named Ruby. Up until a few months prior to the next incident, I'd never met Martha in person. We'd just spoken on the phone.

One night, I was driving home to the cabin, and a deer ran out in front of my car. I swerved and missed the deer but hit a limb which demolished the passenger side of my windshield. It was hard to see after that, and it's already hard to find the cabin's entrance anyway, so I ended up parking my car on the road and just walking a short way to my house.

I got a worried text from Martha the next day asking if I was OK because she'd seen the windshield. I said I was fine, but I'd meet her out at the road to say hi in person. I walked out and finally met Martha, neighbor Jeff, and Alexander. I also met Athena, Jeff's pit bull. Athena blissfully wiggled while I gave her belly rubs right in the middle of the road. I looked at Jeff and kiddingly told him I was going to steal his dog. I didn't really mean it, but that's pretty close to what happened next.

That night I was working at the dining table as usual and had several dog treats on the window sill for the raccoons, but no raccoons came that night. Athena snuck up and ate one of the treats. She looked at me through the window and hesitated as if to say "Am I in trouble?" I smiled at her. She ate the rest of the treats. Then she started whining at the door, so I let her in. And that was the beginning of a very special bond.

While I'm working, she sits right by my side in the daytime, and at night she guards the door. If I'm working in the yard, she comes with me. She barks and chases anything that comes close. She also likes to take naps on the bed.

I normally would not let a dog sleep in my bed, but Athena can. Neighbor Jeff rescued her from a bad situation. Someone kept her in a room with no windows. They also wrapped her tail with a rubber band to "dock" her, so half of her tail rotted off. Jeff didn't want a dog, but he also didn't want her to live like that, so he took her up to the mountain with him. Now she runs free and is a very happy dog. Any animal near Martha, Jeff, or Alexander is happy.

One morning, Martha called and asked me if I wanted to go with her and Alexander to feed Ruby the cow her arthritis medicine.

Sure! It sounded like an adventure.

So they picked me up and we drove a few miles down the road to Benjy's house where Ruby stays. Benjy was Martha's other son who died years ago from cancer at 36 years old.

At Benjy's house, there's a large gate at the road and then a spacious field to the left in the front of the house where Ruby sits. Ruby likes peanut butter and jelly sandwiches, so that's how they get her to eat her medicine. Grape and strawberry. Those are her favorite flavors.

Behind the house is a large lake, and behind that is a handmade wooden fence on the crest of a hill amidst the trees. I asked Martha why they didn't move Ruby over to her house and sell Benjy's.

Well, Ruby cannot be transported, because they can't get her to walk up a ramp onto a platform. Also, more importantly, Benjy is buried inside the wooden fence on the hill. Martha abided by his wishes to die at home and stay at home.

Normally you cannot just bury a body on your own property, but due to his Cherokee Native American heritage, this was allowed.

Her other son Jeff dug the grave and handled the body. Jeff is a good brother and a good son. I cannot imagine having to do all of that, especially in a moment of grief.

Martha told me all of this while we were feeding the catfish in the lake.

Meanwhile, Alexander, the 12 year old, wanted to tell me about anything and everything. He doesn't get to be around other people much. Now all of a sudden with me there, he had someone new to share with. He wanted to play a song for me on his guitar. So we sat by the lake and he played a song that he wrote. It was a prayer to God humbly asking for help. I was crying before he got through the first verse. Like Martha, he has a beautiful, kind heart.

Martha mentioned that she'd never been invited to any of the neighbor's houses. No one did that up there. Well I'm new, and I do invite people over. So I invited Alexander and Martha over for dinner the next night. We had a great time. Martha and I got to talk for a couple of hours, and meanwhile I showed Alexander my new lock picking training kit. He had so much fun with that, and he got really good at it. I ordered one for him to arrive after I left.

Alexander brought me a can safe that he'd made. It's a can of peas that he had emptied so that you can hide valuables in it. I love things like that. I especially love that one since it is a very special and thoughtful gift. He did a really good job smoothing the edges.

Alexander also brought me a welcome mat for my front door that says, "Our Happy Place". And under that, he'd written in black permanent marker "Natalie and Athena". Such a thoughtful and accurate gift.

Neighbor Jeff was also unbelievably kind. He came over with his chainsaw to cut down three trees that were threatening to fall on the house. He also spent at least an hour with the weedeater on the entire yard. When he was done, it looked better than I've ever seen it.

I invited Jeff over for a glass of wine later and he said he'd come over, but first he wanted to show me around in the "side by side".

Sure! Again, it sounded like an adventure.

I had no idea what a side by side was.

It's basically a vehicle that is larger and more powerful than a golf cart, but smaller than a car. We rode for about 20 minutes and then had a glass of wine at my place.

When he left, Athena stayed with me. I'm not sure if I stole her or if she stole me. But she certainly had my heart.

The next morning, I needed to leave to go back to my mom. As I was closing down everything at the cabin and packing the car, Jeff stopped by to get Athena. I hugged him and Athena with tears streaming down my face. I hated leaving the cabin. Our happy place. Natalie and Athena.

And Dad.

35

BACK INTO THE ARENA

I had a job interview in San Francisco scheduled the next week, so I wanted to spend time with Mom before leaving.

I left the cabin and got back to Mom's house late. I slept at the office/garage apartment, but at six a.m., I went over to the house.

Mom: Oh you're up early.

Me: Yep, I'm always up early.

Mom: Oh I thought you'd be asleep, since you sleep in.

Me: [very annoyed] I don't sleep in. I've been working since fou a.m.

We have had this conversation at least a hundred times.

It does not help to get upset about it. I am working on that.

My mom thinks of me as a teenager who sleeps until noon. I WISH I were that person. My reality is that I am awake more hours than I should be. I've had insomnia for decades.

With dementia, losing memory is like an onion. You lose the most recent things first. So my mom can remember her vacations from seventy years ago, but she cannot remember that she told me the same story five minutes ago. She also can't remember that we've had certain conversations a hundred times. And she doesn't think of me as an adult, because, to her, I'm not.

The onion layers are slowly peeling away. Because of that, I have learned to minimize change for her. For instance, she loved using her iPad a year ago, and I bought her an iPhone, since it works basically the same way. She used it then a few times, but now it's confusing. One day she mentioned that several of the house landline phones weren't working, so I told her that she could use her iPhone to make calls if the usual phones aren't working. She wasn't sure about how to use it. (I'd written instructions, but they "disappeared".) Then she asked me

> Mom: "Hey, what is that pink thing that you hold in your hand and talk into?"
>
> Me: "That's my iPhone. You have one too, but yours has flowers on it. You can use it as a phone, just like the land line phone."
>
> Mom: "Oh, that would be useful."

That made me laugh. Yes, it would be very useful. If she would actually use it. I know she'll forget this conversation soon.

She doesn't look at the iPhone as a phone because it doesn't look like the phones she's accustomed to. It doesn't have buttons and cords.

Using old words is another thing that's happening more. We got a new gas heater on the sun porch and she refers to it as a "stove", because that's how they heated their house when she was little - with a stove. So that's what it is to her. She also refers to movies as "pictures".

Old familiar things are best. I eventually learned that I cannot ask her to change her behavior. I have to change mine and meet her where she is. Adapt and compromise.

So I call the heater a stove now too.

36

SOMEONE COULD USE THAT

Years ago, I joked that I had a three-day limit on staying with my parents before I started going crazy. As it is for many people, staying with my parents was like living with roommates that have been pushing your buttons for decades. Consequently, my fuse was short on really silly things sometimes.

In 2003, Mom and I traveled together to England. We had a great trip, but on the first day, we were tired after being on the plane and not sleeping, so I was trying to sleep in our hotel room while Mom was trying to find things in her suitcase. She'd put everything in ziplock bags, and for at least 30 minutes, it was just a constant rustling of plastic.

This was the moment that I suspected that Mom had a ziploc bag problem.

To this day, fifteen years later, if she says, "We can put that in a ziplock bag", my brain spasms a little. You don't have to put every goddamn thing in a ziplock bag. I don't actually say anything like that, because I know it's not a big deal. But it's one of my buttons that gets pushed.

Similarly, we don't have to save all the empty cat treat containers. Also, why do we have fifty Christmas-themed tins in the basement and a hundred wicker baskets? How would we possibly use all of those?

And then there are all the saved Christmas ribbons, gift bags, tissue papers, boxes, and tags. I know a lot of people save things like that, and it's great to re-use what we can, but some of those boxes have been used so many times, the layered tape alone could serve as a Christmas-themed archaeological study.

When my mom and I disagree on throwing things out, she says, "But someone could use that."

No. No they couldn't. No one needs an empty cat treat container. No one wants the old clothes with paint on them that you also do not want. Giving people damaged clothes is not charity.

I understand the tendency to try not to waste things, but there is a limit. As an extreme example, you don't give away your old toothbrush in the hopes that someone can use it. You throw it away. It is OK to throw things away.

Sometimes Mom is worried that someone will break into the house and take things. My thoughts on this are: "Please do! Let me get the door for you. Take as much of this as you want! Can I help you carry these things to your car? Are you free to rob us again tomorrow? My schedule is pretty open, so let's go with what works for you. Do you need any cat treat containers? Wicker baskets? Do you have a truck?"

37

COLORS

When my dad died, my mom really wanted a new car.

No one in our family has ever had a new car, but if it made her happy, then that was fine with me.

She wanted "what all the girls at church have". She also wouldn't let me help, since I'm female, and men buy cars.

Thankfully neighbor Don Holley (a man) knew what "all the girls at church have", so he took her to the Lexus dealership and they came home many hours later with a new car.

From San Francisco, I called and asked her if she loved it, and she burst into tears.

> Me: What happened? Are you ok? Is the car ok? What's wrong?

> Mom: [Sobbing] It's not yellow enough.

I wanted to be there with her to give her a hug and tell her that it's just a car. You can take it back. You can get a more yellow one.

She thought she picked out one car and then they gave her car to someone else.

It's just paranoia.

Sometimes I don't know what is real. In that moment though, it didn't matter. It's real to her.

I told her that sometimes light on car paint is different at different times of day, so maybe it just looks different right now, but it will look right in the morning. Car paint does do that. She seemed somewhat reassured with that and stopped crying.

I called her first thing in the morning. She was dressed and ready to take it back. Her plan was to go by herself.

Me: How are you going to get home?

Mom: ...I hadn't thought about that.

Me: OK, can you please charge your phone and take it with you? Can Don help?

Mom: I'll call a taxi. (Alabama is not a place where people call a taxi.)

I called Don.

Me: Is there any chance she picked out a car and they gave her a different one.

Don: No.

Me: Ok, well I don't think we're going to talk her into thinking that is the case. I hate to ask you to help her again today, but she's about to go down there by herself. Can you please go with her?

Of course he did.

She came home with a red car. Not at all yellow. I didn't point that out.

I'm just happy that she's happy.

38

STILL GRIEVING

I think about my dad a lot. I can't control losing him, so I compensate by cleaning. I can control the cleaning.

I find myself washing the windows at his office at three a.m. I clean the cabin every time I go there too.

I wish I'd done that when he was with me. I know it is an act of love now. I love the office and the cabin, because they were his.

I really wish we'd spent more time together. But we didn't. I worked too much.

I wish I'd taken every one of his calls instead of letting it go to voicemail.

He visited me once in California. We had a fun time. His plane landed in the afternoon. I picked him up and the first thing he wanted to do was to go to the cemetary where admirals Nimitz and Spruance were buried. Sure.

Dad was quirky sometimes, but always a scholar. He'd been reading about these admirals, so we went and found these headstones at the cemetary. Then we drove around San Francisco, and later that night we picked up some food to take home and drank three bottles of wine while we talked until very late. It was one of my favorite conversations with Dad. He told me that he so loved Mom, and that part of what he loves is that she is always so positive. And she is.

I also miss my mom, even though physically she's here. I wish I'd spent more time with her too, before this shift.

Part of what hurts with Mom is that sometimes she is mostly there. Other times, she is just not herself. It's hard to lose her, get her back, lose her again, get her back. She's both here and not here. You never know which mom you're going to get. How many years of this are ahead? I hope many. I hope none.

The only thing I can do is breathe and love her no matter what.

39

WITH THESE MEN PRESENT

When we thought my dad was days from dying, we rushed to write legal documents, and we scrambled to assemble documents with the help of several very close family friends.

I greatly appreciated having that help. At the same time, I strongly objected to the language in almost everything we had to sign. There was nothing legally wrong with the documents. My issue was that many of them started, "With these men present, ..."

Excuse me? With these MEN present?

DO YOU SEE WHO IS HERE SIGNING THINGS?!

Women.

Who is on the Powers of Attorney for my parents?

Women.

Who arranged for the paperwork to get done? Who gathered everyone?

Women. Women. Women. Women.

Strong women are present. My mom is here. I am here. Dotsy is here. Dotsy's daughter Maggie is here. WE are holding down the fort here. WE are the strong ones right now. And we're signing papers that start with "With these MEN present"?

Can we change it to "With these WOMEN present?" Or just take out that whole phrase? What century are we in right now?

And if we're going to adjust the phrasing, could we change it to "With these unbelievably accomplished and beautiful women present", or "with these goddesses present", or "with these kind souls present"? Any of that would have been more palatable.

Sure, men helped us and were also present, and I appreciated all of that help, but I still hated that phrasing. It was unecessary and anti-quated. I kept my mouth shut because I didn't want to have to redo all the paperwork and delay the process. Ladies often go along with such things so they don't ruffle feathers. Right then I wasn't worried about being a lady. I only went along with it for the expediancy of getting things done.

Real women just get things done even when tradition is outdated and stupid. Thankfully my family is full of real women. We got it all done, beyond just paperwork. And I know that we got things done with these WOMEN present.

40

BECOMING THE ADULT

Before he died, Dad handled all the financial things. After he died, I shifted all the assets they had to a local bank so that Mom would be able to walk in the branch and actually talk with someone she knows.

After meeting with the bankers, she said she felt like I was the parent now. I said "No. We are both adults, and I'm just helping. We're getting through this together. We met them together."

Then there was the issue of keeping her safe. She thinks I bugged the house. She's right. I did.

They say people go through a second childhood in old age. I think that's a miscategorization of what's happening now, but our roles did flip. I tried to become the best actress on the planet to pretend that she was in charge.

I wanted her to stay strong and healthy, so I let her do things that I maybe shouldn't have. It's a fine line between encouraging vitality and managing safety. I'm sure I got it wrong a lot, but I tried.

She is losing cognitive functioning in parts of her brain that controls emotion, logic, and judgement. Her emotions are erratic. Meanwhile, she's frustrated with things that she used to do but that are now challenging. Like how to use the remote control for the TV.

Losing my dad was shattering and overwhelming for me at first. Everything dad handled suddenly got poured into my cup, and with mom slowly transitioning to needing more help, it feels like a steady drip of new responsibility. I rearranged my life to handle all of that. And I'm so glad I did.

41

MY INERTIA

If you want to get something done, give it to a busy person.

An object in motion stays in motion.

Most of my days in life have been busy and productive, but when I started staying with my mom everything changed.

I got stuck.

For so long I felt, "I am not in motion." Will someone please make me go to the gym.

I got very stuck physically and mentally.

42

GRABBING LIFE BACK

One of the last things my dad said while in the hospital was, "Enjoy your life, Nat."

I think about that often. I wonder what he'd think about my life now.

I know it doesn't make sense to be concerned about the judgement of someone not even alive. Part of my enjoying life is letting go of feeling judged at all. Thankfully, I've made some progress on this.

I've started saying to people giving unsolicited advice that I don't agree with, "Thank you for your opinion." For the more egregious oversteps, I tell them, "Thank you. You are invited to leave."

I've gotten better at pushing people away when their comments are consistently judgemental and unhelpful. I recognize that they don't mean to be hurtful. That doesn't mean I have to talk with them though.

Then there's finding actual joy.

Where is joy for me? Dancing, the gym, connecting with friends and family, seeing art, making art, learning, cooking, being at the cabin with Athena, doing anything that makes Mom happy.

I also have fun playing pool at Murios, a bar near my apartment in San Francisco. I started playing a year ago, and not only do I love the geometry of it, I also love that anyone can play, and I meet a diverse set of people when I'm there. Since it's San Francisco, I meet a lot of people in the tech-industry. But one day someone new showed up. He worked in construction, and he told me his whole family was killed by a drunk driver. He went to the sentencing at court, and said he got off three rounds before they tackled him. I don't know how he got a gun into a courthouse or how he did not go to prison. But the jury sided with him. You never know who you'll meet, and that's part of why I like the game.

Connecting with people is my biggest joy in life.

I look for ways to connect with my mom. I am losing her. My mom keeps leaving messages on my cell phone. Except it's not my cell phone. I have no idea who she's calling.

One connection that was especially beautiful during all of the parent chaos was an interaction that happened during a Lyft ride to the hospital to see my father. The driver of course knew we were going to a hospital, and he told me he was a minister in addition to being a driver. After hearing me explain my situation, he asked if he could pray with me. I probably do not have the exact same beliefs that this man had, but I appreciated his intentions, and I could tell that he meant kindness and love. So we prayed in the car. Just when I thought San Francisco was the most crazy city, Birmingham, Alabama brings out the weirdness in a most loving way!

43

THE GOOD MOMENTS WITH MOM

I loved spending time with Mom. She was always up for an adventure, so I took her to sushi one day. She loved it. So we went another day. And then we'd been so many times, the staff started giving her welcoming hugs.

One memory that I love is Thanksgiving 2018. Our big family meal was Friday instead of Thursday, because my cousins are both doctors, and they worked Thanksgiving Thursday. But Mom wanted to go out and eat anyway on Thursday. So we got in the car and drove until we finally found a place that was open. A taqueria.

We were the only customers there. We ordered a quesadilla and guacamole, and both of them were really bad. I didn't say anything. Mom is generally positive and rarely complains, but after a few bites, she said the meat was tough. I nodded yes and smiled. Also, how do you make guacamole wrong? I don't know, but it was not good. When mom and I got into the car, she looked at me and said, "That was the worst meal I've ever had." I agreed, and we laughed so hard.

I am thankful that I have a funny memory of a terrible meal with Mom.

44

HOSPICE

A few years ago I wanted to paint my kitchen walls white, and I stopped into a paint store for white paint.

Well do you want cotton? More of an alpaca? Cloud?

What? I just wanted white paint. I had never considered that there are shades of white.

There are shades of everything.

"Midnight black" is an interesting color to me. At midnight, it's not actually black. Sometimes it's a beautiful sea of stars.

This is how I see hospice. A lot of people think it would be dark, but it can also be both dark and beautiful.

I started volunteering with a hospice service about a year after my dad passed away. Not because I was looking for it. I was simply looking for volunteer opportunities and hospice volunteering fit my schedule of being available for two months in Alabama and then away for two months while I was in California. The hospice service also really needed people. I guess it's hard to find people to help with that kind of work.

The people you visit are expected to live less than six months.

I grew up volunteering, and have worked with kids, underpriviledged families, animals, etc. But this is by far the most meaningful to me. I know how much it meant to our family when we had people helping us in the last days with my dad.

And this service helps people who really have no one else.

It isn't depressing for me. It's kindness and connection. It's a sincere caring towards someone I just met. And I know I will lose them. Or they might lose me. But that is every relationship.

I lost my dad, and now am losing my mother, so I feel girded now on losing people that I care about.

Jerry (not my uncle) was my favorite to visit, because he needed the most help. He had no family, and all he could say was "Yeah".

Are you cold? Yeah. Are you too warm? Yeah.

He had experienced so many seizures that he couldn't say anything other than "Yeah". So there was no way to know what he wanted, thought, or needed. So I just sat with him and held his hand and talked to him in a very one-sided conversation. I showed him pretty pictures on my phone. I brought him flowers to smell.

One day, I told him I had to go back to San Francisco, but I was looking forward to seeing him again when I came back. He was so thin.

He died two weeks later.

Yeah.

45

THIS BODY GOT ME TO BEING RIGHT HERE

When you stop working out hard, your body shape shifts. But I'll tell you this, I wanted to be in really good shape to help my mom, and I certainly was. I picked her up more than once, and carried her.

I am still strong. I just don't look like it. This bothered me for a long time. And then I just decided that I don't have to look a certain way right now. I feel beautiful because of my choices.

This body expressed love, sacrifice, caring, and determination. This body got the important things done.

46

MARTHA

I mentioned Martha before. She's one of my neighbors at the cabin. We now talk on the phone often, and sometimes when I'm at the cabin she comes over to say hello.

When Martha visits, she might drive her car over, but she's just two houses down, so sometimes she drives her golf cart.

Picture Martha in the driver's seat of the golf cart, a cat on the seat next to her, a dog on the floorboard in front of the cat, a dog on the back of the cart, and eight more dogs trailing behind as if it's a dog parade. It's hilarious! And you hear them coming because there are hound dogs in the bunch leading the parade, so they get all the other dogs rowled up.

It's an absolute joy to see them running down the driveway.

And then, if I don't close the doors, ooooh, it's a dog party inside. They're running and jumping, grabbing food off the counter, jumping on the couch, and digging in the trash. They're just being dogs, so I'm never mad, but I've learned to keep the doors closed. I love them all though.

They need homes, and Martha is so kind-hearted to have taken in these sweeties that were abandoned.

Martha strongly believes in God, but she doesn't go to church. Her faith is strong enough at home, and in her experience, at church, people talk behind your back when you wear the wrong things (She's right). She sees no reason to dress up. She spends her money on helping animals that she rescues, rather than buying clothes just to fit in at church. I love her. I AM her. In too many ways to count.

I hope over time, I'll become even more like her. More nice, and more mean too. I hope I have her wisdom one day.

Again, I'm not glad that my dad died. But if he hadn't died when he did, I probably wouldn't have met Martha. And her friendship has been one of the most wonderful blessings in my life.

One of the kindest things she said helps me still. I told her I had so many regrets about taking care of Dad. I think about how I could have maybe done it better. She took a long pause to try to phrase it. She had taken care of her father in his final phase too.

"If we had no regrets, then compassion is gone."

To my wise friend, Martha, thank you.

47

CHARLIE

Charlie was my dad's best friend. They were in the Navy together. Roommates in Charlston, South Carolina. They went to the Navy's nuclear power school together too. And then they went to Harvard Business School together. They also almost got arrested once for shooting a roadsign with a pistol while on a roadtrip, but somehow they lucked out when the patrol officer didn't arrest them. Those two also lucked out by just knowing each other.

As a kid, I didn't know most of my dad's friends who called our house, but I knew Charlie. Dad was always really happy to hear from "C-squared". His initials are C.C., a math joke that I didn't get until later. They also had a long-running inside joke about a coffee pot that got damaged while they were roommates, with both blaming each other for decades, so they'd occasionally teasingly mail each other a coffee pot.

When Dad was sick, there was a point when there was no more teasing and joking. He didn't have the energy for it.

After Dad moved from the hospital to home with hospice, I called Charlie and asked if he wanted to fly down to say goodbye to his friend. I knew we only had days.

Charlie didn't want to. He didn't want to remember his friend like that.

At the time, I was surprised, but later I understood.

I asked Dad if others could come see him "to say hi", and he didn't want anyone to visit. I now recognize that he didn't want people to see him that way. Even if it meant never seeing them again.

I respected his wishes, but I didn't understand, because I think I'd want to see everyone I love if I were dying. But those are MY preferences, not his.

I am glad that he could tell me what he wanted. Maybe he was embarassed. Maybe he felt like less of himself. Maybe he needed time to make peace with what was happening.

Or, maybe you don't want people coming over and crying about your dying before you actually die.

Charlie probably played that right. No one saw Dad like that except me, Mom, and our hospice care.

I was there for all of it, and I never thought of him as weak or lesser than anything. To me, he was strong until the last breath.

But I now understand C-squared. You don't want your military buddies to see you in a hospital gown with a diaper. I get it.

Charlie knew my father wouldn't want to be remembered that way, and Charlie was right. That was the best gift he could have ever given my dad. That and the coffee pot.

48

C-SQUARED

Charlie came to the funeral. He also stayed in touch with me afterward. I was already close with him as a second father figure. He lives in Chicago in a beautiful apartment just off of Michigan Avenue with gorgeous views of the city and Lake Michigan. The last time I was in Chicago for work, I made sure to stop by to see him, and we had so much fun talking. He insisted on calling my dad, who I was SURE was sleeping at ten p.m., but we called anyway and got my mom, and Charlie asked her to tell my dad we'd spent $30 on a hamburger. We hadn't, but he just wanted to make Dad gasp at the thought. We laughed a lot that night, tickled at what Dad would think about a $30 hamburger.

Charlie and I talked a lot after Dad died. He'd lost his wife many years ago to cancer so he knew what it was to experience a profound loss, and he knew I was on an emotional rollercoaster. He was also preparing himself to become a coach for people retiring and going through the retirement transition, so he suggested that he could maybe practice that with me. I wasn't retiring, but I was sure going through a transition. So we ended up talking about once a month, and in those conversations he'd ask me questions. I'd generally just spew thoughts that I couldn't say to other people. Frustrations, fears, angers, insecurities, joys, accomplishments...

One day, C-Squared asked me, "If your Dad were here right now with you, what would you say? What would you do?"

Of course I teared up in answering.

I'd run to him and hug him. I'd say "I love you" and "Thank you for all that you did for me and Mom." And "How the hell do you keep the office cool in the summer? The air conditioners do not work!". Charlie and I laughed.

I'd ask Dad to tell me all about the birds that he loved to watch so much.

We both always liked animals. And animals liked him. All the cats we had over the years adopted HIM. They just showed up, and he was nice to them, so they stayed.

He loved Mamma Cat the most. There was a severe snowstorm in Birmingham in 1993, and during that storm a mother cat and her two tiny kittens crawled out of the snowy woods next to our house. She was feral but shivering and desperate, so she let Dad help her. We found homes for the kittens eventually, but Mamma cat stayed. She eventually got really sick though, and Dad had to use a needle to drain fluid from her belly every day. He tried to save her, but she died on Thanksgiving day right before all of our family came over for the meal.

I only saw my Dad cry twice that I can recall: When our neighbor-friend across the street died. And when that cat died.

Dad really struggled to say the blessing over our meal that day. I know he wanted to just get up from the table and go to the office and cry. If I could talk to him, I'd tell him that I should have said the blessing that day.

I'd also tell him about the cabin, and how I love it and how I love the neighbors and how I leave dog treats on the window sills for the raccoons and their little paws come up over the edge while I'm working. It's adorable.

I'd tell him I miss him.

I'd tell him not to worry about me and Mom. We're a team, and I'm going to do everything in my power to keep her safe and happy. He did a good job with that for forty years for both of us. Now it's my turn.

I would tell him that I'm so proud of him.

49

SOCKS

When you step in a puddle and your socks get wet, the best thing about that is that they're wet.

You can now walk through another puddle without worrying about getting your socks wet. They're already wet. You can't make them MORE wet. It's liberating.

Dealing with my mom's dementia has been like that for me.

Stepping in a puddle, at first, when you're feeling the water seep in, it feels like something to resist or try to stop. But then, it happens anyway. So now you can take on another puddle. Now you can walk into a creek, a river, an ocean.

Recognizing what was happening to my mom was really difficult, but it gave me a new kind of confidence. My job is to protect her. My feet are wet. I'm not afraid of it anymore.

When I first realized what was happening with my mom, I was sad and in shock. Now, I've learned how to navigate this ocean with her. The winds and the tides are constantly changing. You are in the ocean. There is no stability. Your socks are wet.

You can try to go back inside and change, but you're still going to be right back in the ocean.

Just go with it.

"Be water, my friend." ~ Bruce Lee

50

THE CABIN

Being at the cabin, I am becoming a different person by learning and really appreciating nature and new friendships.

I feel like I've been getting a PhD in practical skills for the past few years while managing repairs and improvements at the cabin. I've learned more about trees, gravel, propane, ticks, and septic tanks than I ever thought I would need to know. For instance, pine burns quickly. Oak does not. People who use fireplaces a lot avoid pine because it gives off resin which can catch your house on fire. There is a squirrel hunting season. Mice and insects don't like peppermint smells. Snakes don't like ammonia. Good snakes keep away the bad snakes. Coiled snakes are in a position to launch, but the ones that are more straight can't jump at you.

I'm not glad that my dad passed away, but that earthquake in our family led me to make choices that let me be closer to my mom and to develop knowledge that I would have never had otherwise. I've also developed friendships and connections that I never would have had otherwise.

Neighbors Martha, Jeff, and Alexander are part of the steel net that caught me. There isn't a word strong enough to say how much I appreciate them. They have shown me love like family. (The good kind of family. Not the ones you gossip about and hope they can't make it to Thanksgiving.)

Jeff is really good at a lot of things, and one night about midnight I called him for an unusual "Help!". An armadillo had wandered into my bathroom (I had left the doors open for the dog), and it was hiding behind the toilet. My friend Danny was on the phone with me first and he'd told me to get the broom and "just swish it". "Swish it." Danny assures me that they do not jump. Ok, so I get up on top of the toilet with a broom and with one foot on the toilet and one on the sink for stability, I swished it. And it tried to jump up the wall (I saw it! Danny was wrong!). I'm screaming, and it ran behind the hot water heater, where it is now stuck.

Danny said to grab its tail. Um, NO. Did you miss the class on how not to handle cornered animals?

Also, in my free time, while I was trying to figure out what to do with my bathroom armadillo, I researched online and found that armadillos are one of the few animals that can carry leprosy. I'm definitely not touching it.

I swear to god if anyone else ever tells me to just swish it, I'm going to lose it.

So again, this is very late at night, and I wake Jeff. The conversation was basically, "Hey Jeff, sorry to call so late, but there's an armadillo in my bathroom." He says, "Swish it with a broom." I didn't lose it then, but I knew I wasn't going to swish it again. It was stuck. So I just left the door open with hopes it would meander out on its own. It didn't. About seven a.m. I called Jeff again. He came over, grabbed it by the tail, and put it outside where it waddled off. So far, Jeff does not have leprosy.

Martha is Jeff's mom. Since I started spending time at the cabin, Martha and I talk just about every day.

She has so many fun phrases. I write them down sometimes. Imagine this in a Dolly Parton accent:

> I wouldn't piss on him if he was on fire (There's an awful person nearby that hurts dogs. We both hate him.)

> Grinning like a big possum (Alexander got a package he was excited about.)

> She wouldn't bite a hot biscuit (Athena the dog)

> Like a chicken on a junebug (Going after something with determination. You're finxin' to go to war!)

> Fine as frogs' hair! (You're doing great)

> You're choppin' in high cotton! (You're having a great day, and you don't have to bend over all day.)

Martha is in her 70's with a wealth of wisdom, and has taught me so much.

I can't recount everything she's taught me, but just one thing is that if you want a big tree to grow, you cut the small trees near it, so the big one gets the nutrients. Makes sense. I now do the same with flowers. Cut the parts you don't want so the rest can thrive. I think that logic equally applies to life, especially how to spend your time, and who you spend it with.

51

CHARLA & NOT WALLOWING

Charla is one of my good friends from California. We met because we were both looking for a running partner. I remember the first time we met, it was six a.m., and I texted her to look for the brunette in hot pink shoes. We've stayed close friends for years, even after she moved to Texas.

She lost a baby in December, two years after she moved. She knew the baby had a very slim chance of living. The doctors said it likely had Down Syndrome and also had a heart defect. It died inside her. Her mom was with her when they had to go to the hospital to induce a labor process that ended with Charla holding her baby, Ciela.

She would have been a great mom. She was already a great mom, because she had every chance to terminate a difficult and risky pregnancy, but she wanted to give Ceilal a chance, and she did that.

Charla couldn't talk about it at first, so my card to her said, please let me be first in line to punch anyone in the face that says "She's in a better place" or "Everything happens for a reason".

Maybe her baby IS in a better place, and maybe everything DOES happen for a reason, but saying it is not making anyone feel better right now. And I know that from having it said to me. I don't think losing my dad happened in order to teach me what words to say or not say to someone grieving, but it did teach me at least not to say those things. And I'm glad that through my loss I can more closely connect with my friend in her time of loss.

One night between Christmas and New Years, I had a chance to talk with Charla for two hours.

Aside from a lot of things to laugh about, she'd just been to a grief therapy group, so we talked about that.

She noticed that some of the people who go there have been going for years, and she wasn't judging them, but it seemed like a long time to linger in the suffering. It was not something she aspired to being. She mentioned this to her therapist who said that some people define themselves by their grief.

Sometimes I feel guilty of that, because a lot of my sentences start off with, "After Dad died…". But I don't think that's defining myself with grief. I think it is a reference point. It's sort of like if there had been a tornado that scrambled my life, I'd probably say, "After the tornado, we now do certain things differently".

That is true for me after losing my dad. And it is also true for Charla after losing her baby. She said one day, "What else in life could change your life that drastically?" And then we laughed as she said sex wasn't a hard thing to give up (which I would never in 1000 years have expected to hear from her feminist sex-positive friendly adventurous-in-every-way self). She is fine, but she abstained for a while for various reasons.

Charla also decided to use her brief experience with motherhood as a way to give. She pumped milk for several months and donated her breast milk to others who needed it.

That's not wallowing. That's warrior strength.

And after trying again, she now has a healthy beautiful baby girl to whom she is a wonderful mom!

52

STOICISM

Stoicism doesn't mean not caring. It means not letting other people's emotions and judgements throw you.

I liken it to riding a motorcycle. You cannot let outside influences distract you. You have to focus on what matters.

I know where I'm going. I know what I'm doing. Unless something arises that actually matters, I'm not changing my course.

You can acknowledge emotions and let others' river of emotion pass, but you don't have to take it on as yours. It will flow past.

And you don't have to defend yourself when people say things that don't matter.

After my father died, I spent a lot of emotional capital on things that don't matter. What other people say to me. What other people think of me. My extended family. My mother. People who once I thought were friends.

Feeling judged is new territory for me. When it felt unfair, it was worse. But I now see that as either misunderstanding or insecurity within the person saying things that felt unkind.

Thankfully I have a great therapist and great friends who have helped me adjust to this shift in how I think of my mom. She is not a child. She is also not my mother. Her feelings matter. But I can choose to be stoic. That does not mean that I don't care. I do. That means that her feelings do not guide me and my actions.

53

YES, GIRL!

Shane is a man that looks like a lion if you could dress a lion in 70's clothes. He has a mane of red hair, always wears a leather jacket and a gauzy white shirt, and he has a commanding booming voice.

The man has an interesting resume.

He was formerly a radio announcer, then he was a marine with the U.S. military, and then he took care of his grandma in her final two years.

He and I talked about the challenges of taking care of someone with dementia, and one of the best pieces of advice he gave me was to always walk into the room happy. If you're upset about something else outside of that room, then they will feel it but not know how to deal with it. If you're frustrated or mad at them, they will feel it and then will feel upset too and likely will feel confused.

Just walk in happy. Every. Time.

Fake it if you have to.

Athena dog reminds me of this lesson all the time. Sometimes she likes to run for fun in Birmingham, and I have to go get her from a neighbor's yard. When I'm walking toward her, if she thinks I'm mad at her, she runs further. If I talk to her with a friendly happy voice, she'll come to me, and I can attach her leash.

She mimics my emotions at home too. At the cabin, when she hears a noise, her ears will perk up, and I'll say with urgency, "Go get 'em! Go get 'em!" And she runs around the woods like a racehorse. I'm pretty sure 90% of the time the noise is from racoons. The other 10% is probably leaves.

My favorite connection with Athena though is saying, "Yes girrrl!" It sounds like squirrel, but it's girrrl. I just say it happily when I see her, when she wakes up, when we jump in the car... any time. And her tail just starts wagging. She's such a happy dog when I start the happy.

Athena helps me to remember that it doesn't matter what happened yesterday or an hour ago. If I walk into Mom's room happy, Mom reflects it back.

54

FRIED PICKLES

What are summer teeth? Well it's when some are there and some are not. Summerteeth.

Fort Payne, Alabama prides itself in being the "Sock Capital of the World". They have the finest Applebees around, and right down the street from Wal-Mart is Jefferson's, where my friend Wally and I ended up ordering dirty martinis after our trip to Wal-Mart, which is the closest place to get provisions.

The bartender at Jefferson's was really sweet, and the fried pickles were great, but that was the absolute worst dirty martini I've ever had in my life. My friend Wally and I sipped on them a while and chatted with the man next to us. He suggested that we order a Carl's Special, which is the local version of the long island iced tea. We were halfway into the first one when we learned that HE was THE CARL. And the stories commenced.

He had a limo service for a few years. He reports that the rounchiest crowds he ever had in his limos were always the women. "You get 15 women drunk and all hell breaks loose."

He told us about the ladies that decorate his Christmas tree wearing only Santa hats and socks.

Carl had all the connections.

Eventually I mentioned that my septic tank at the cabin had a problem. Carl told us about Donnie's septic service, and I called Donnie the next morning. Unfortunately his truck was heavy, and my driveway was waterlogged from a lot of rain, so his truck got stuck in the mud. He called everyone he knew with machinery to get it out, and every time a friend called he always answered loudly with just, "WHAT?" Even when he was frustrated, he was hilarious. He also called dogs "crotch sniffers".

At Applebees, later that day, a guy named Roy knew about Donnie too. He said, one time, Donnie serviced an establishment and expected payment on the spot. He emptied their septic tank, and when they didn't pay him, he put back the septic contents and asked them to call him when they had the money.

WHAT?!

I like Donnie.

55

MISS DELORES

The idea of volunteering in hospice work may sound sad, but it rarely is. It's simply spending time with people who appreciate companionship and who may need help with things.

I think online dating prepared me for hospice work. You meet someone, maybe hold their hand. And then you don't see them again. And you wish them well.

I hope I see Miss Delores again though. She was 92 and deaf. I visited her so that her daughter could go to the doctor.

Miss Delores slept most of the time I was at her house, but she woke up around eleven a.m. and wanted to make lunch for herself. She had a notepad, and she asked me about my family.

I'd brought Athena who was perfectly happy in the car, and to me Athena counted as family, so I mentioned her. Miss Delores wanted to meet her. So I brought Athena on a leash up to the porch, so Miss Delores could pet her.

I don't know much sign language, but Miss Delores signed "I love you" as I was leaving. I signed the same back. I know that one.

If you don't know it, close your hand completely, extend your thumb and index finger to make an L shape, and then add your pinkie up.

Love.

56

TURNING INTO MY DAD

That's what it feels like sometimes, turning into my dad. I've assumed his role in taking care of my mom and the house and the cabin. I make sure the smoke detectors are working, pour the water out of the dehumidifiers in the basement when it floods, take care of the insurance papers and taxes, pressure wash the front patio when the algae builds up on it.

Dad would have done all of that.

But I'm not my dad because I'm doing it my way. I have technology on my side. I have alerts on my phone when the car moves. I can check on my mom with cameras in the house.

My father was a really smart man. I wish we had spent more time together, because I think we would have learned from each other. I'm learning from him now though. I can see how he thought by seeing how he built the cabin. He thought all of it out in detail.

When I first got to the cabin after he passed, I found the dehumidifier in the middle of the room, with a hose going to the shower drain. I put it away and forgot about it. And then in the fall when I went back, there was mold all over my boots that I'd left.

He had the dehumidifier for a reason.

I ordered two more.

I'm not turning into my dad. I'm understanding my dad.

57

I DID TELL YOU

It's been raining for weeks with few breaks. My mom's basement floods, and at 82 years old she's down there sweeping water into a drain pipe under the unfinished sink. There are two dehumidifiers in the basement, but she doesn't remember to use them. Even if she did, she'd have to empty the heavy gallons of water every few hours when the flooding happens. I decided that we needed two new dehumidifiers with a hose that empties directly into the drain pipe, so they'd always be on, and she wouldn't have to empty anything, and she wouldn't have so much to sweep.

So I ordered the dehumidifiers one morning. And then I went to the cabin, because I wanted to take Athena back to her dad, Jeff. Before I left, I told Mom that some boxes with dehumidifiers would be arriving while I was gone. And also a harness for Athena.

And then I got the phone call. WHAT ARE YOU ORDERING? ALL OF THESE BOXES ARE HERE AND THEY'RE HEAVY. IS THIS GOING ON MY CREDIT CARD?

(First of all, she doesn't have a credit card, and all of it went on mine.)

"I ordered dehumidifiers for your house. For the basement because it floods when it rains."

And she said, "Well I wish you'd told me."

"I DID TELL YOU!" is what I wanted to say. Because I did. But instead I said, "I'm sorry." And that was also true. Because in her mind, I didn't tell her.

58

WALLY

Wally and I met at the only place in Mentone, Alabama that serves wine. It was a dry county a year prior, so freely available wine within 15 minutes was a new luxury. I was there having dinner at the bar with a friend Meredith who'd come up to visit me and to cut trees with chainsaws for a few days.

Meredith and I were covered in sawdust, but we went to dinner like that, because that's absolutely acceptable in the country. Wally was sitting on the other side of Meredith, but I leaned over and said, "Are you drinking wine out of a plastic cup?" I was just teasing him, a total stranger.

After a few minutes of talking he said his dad died just a few weeks prior to that, and he was there to take care of the cabins that his dad rented out. He's from Alabama but now lives in Miami. Having lost my dad and also having this city/country dual life, I gave him my business card and wrote - "If you ever need anything or just want some company up here."

He texted us before Meredith and I got home just saying it was really nice to meet us. Two days later, Wally and I met for dinner at 5:30 at the Wildflower Cafe. Athena rode with me and stayed in the car. She rode with me almost everywhere then.

Everything closes at eight p.m. in Mentone, but I really wanted to keep talking. So I invited Wally to my house. We talked until three a.m. with Athena sitting in the middle of the couch between us.

And then the next night we were on the phone for hours.

And then he stayed with me for two days, because the cabins that his dad rented out were booked for Valentine's weekend.

Wally fixed many things around my cabin. He also met Martha, the neighbor, Ruby the cow, and spent time with Alexander, the 12 year old next door. Whatever this was, it was good.

One night we ended up in the hot tub at one of his cabins. It was snowing and freezing, but I did have a hat on.

And then he needed to go south toward his brother, so he came home to Birmingham with me for a few days, and he met my mom.

My mom loved Wally. Until she didn't. As Wally would nautically say, "Stand by".

59

THE CEILING FANS

Wally is really great at fixing things. His profession is as a maritime captian of large vessels. As he put it, you are in a floating city and you're out there alone, so if problems arise, you learn to fix things.

So he saw my mom's two ceiling fans on her porch where she spends 90% of her waking hours, and they were clearly not working correctly.

I know that the best way to handle changing anything within the house is to wait until she goes to church, and then make changes, and quickly get out of the house.

That is not what happened.

The wiring for these fans is nearly 90 years old. Wally had no idea that this would be the mess that it became. Something that should take a couple of hours took three days. Three days of Wally standing on a ladder holding up something heavy, listening to my mom asking the same questions15 times. He was so physically and emotionally drained. Mom was sweet though. She tried to give him coffee and cereal in the mornings, and she made snacks for him. She told me she really liked him. She appreciated all of that work.

At the end of day two Wally had one fan fully operational! YES! We all celebrated with high fives. I joked, "And now you get to do it again!" Thankfully the second one was much faster.

When it was 95% done, we were missing wire nuts for the ends of the electrical connections. Wally wanted it to be safe and done correctly.

I KNEW he needed a break so I suggested we start back again in the morning, and I asked him if he wanted to take a shower (I knew he did, because he'd told me, but I wanted Mom to hear the conversation). Him: YES!

Mom suggested that he take one upstairs in the main house. It had to be in the main house, because there wasn't a shower in the garage apartment.

And then I got the call. Mom wants to know why I have men taking showers in the house. Why doesn't he go to his house. Why don't I stay in a hotel if I want to be with a man instead of having someone stay in my "daddy's office".

I'm 42 years old right now, and my own mother is now slut-shaming me even though I'm perfectly capable of having a man stay in my presence and not sleep with him.

Worse than that, she's not respecting my friend, who is helping her by making her house safe. He's worked for THREE days, and she's mad that he's taking a shower.

Worse than that, she doesn't remember that this man is helping her.

Worse than that, I'm angry at her, even though she can't help this.

It's not her fault. It's not her fault. I love her. Repeat repeat repeat.

But what did I do? I walked over to the house and knocked on the bathroom door and explained through the door to Wally that Mom was upset that he was there and there might be some drama, but I made sure he knew he didn't do anything wrong.

And then I went downstairs. I was so angry. I just said, "I have one question" pointing to the ceiling fan that was 95% finished but with exposed wires, "Do you want this finished or not?"

Mom: "No, I'll take care of it."

Me: "OK"

She can't take care of this! You're going to have exposed wires on your ceiling. Are you CRAZY?

Yes, she IS crazy. Welcome to dementia.

I started boxing up all the tools.

I had to make many trips to the tool shed because there was so much there, and she kept closing the door. But I needed it open. So at some point I opened the door and screamed, "I'm not finished yet!" And then I threw a bowl on the floor which shattered.

I swept up the bowl remnants. I took out her trash. I made sure her basement wasn't flooded.

She looked at Wally with disdain when he left. He offered to come back in the morning. Mom: "That won't be necessary." This. This to the man that has spent three days helping you. She was holding the flashlight for him to see into the ceiling. She loves Wally. And now she thinks he's a stranger?

What is happening? This isn't my mom.

It's hard. I'm both angry and sad. I'm more sad. The anger is just momentary. She can't help it.

Wally and I went to dinner. We were both hurt and stunned. Mom was fine and then suddenly she wasn't. Wally said, "Now I really understand what you're going through." I am not sure anyone saw and felt it more than he did.

I am so sorry that my friend had to feel this.

It's a nightmare. Imagine having a car that is perfect 95% of the time, but 5% of the time it severely shocks you when you touch it. That is what walking into Mom's house feels like. You are rolling the dice. You never know which mom you're going to get.

Wally was afraid to go back over to Mom's house, but he told me it was a security risk to leave it unfinished. He asked me to talk with her. I said no. I've learned to leave her alone.

In the morning, after the shower incident the previous night, Mom called me. She asked when Wally could come back. Maybe he could "work us in", as if he's a worker and not my very kind friend.

He fixed it. Of course he did. He's a good guy.

I have to integrate her decline into my life and expectations.

60

THE LEAF BLOWER

Today was another hard one with Mom.

The obsession with colors persists (remember the car not being yellow enough?).

Today she wanted me to move a section of very heavy stones because some were not the right color of grey. They were a little "too orangey".

I did not move the rocks. I'm strong, but I know that moving them would be challenging and possibly hurt me. Hopefully she'll forget about that in a couple of days. Probably not, but my therapist told me that I can't let the whims of someone unreasonable dictate how I prioritize my time or how I feel. I don't have to move the rocks. But I probably will if it keeps bothering her, if only to stop her from doing it herself.

Too late.

She did it anyway. She ended up hurt and in bed for a week.

She wants to be independent, but she has a warped sense of what she can do, so she ends up doing things that injure her or at least put her at risk. She won't wait and let other people help.

It must be hard for her to have a brain that twists reality. It's hard to feel a loss of control. It's hard for me to erect barriers. There are no easy answers because sometimes she's fine, and then two hours later, she's not.

I struggle to constantly muster patience. I know the things she does aren't her fault. I know she's not trying to make things hard for me, so I feel guilty for feeling frustrated. All of it makes me not want to spend time with her though, which further makes me sad and feeling guilty, because I probably don't have much time left with her. I tell myself that she's not my mom anyway at this point, which further makes me sad. It's hard to stay happy and joyful and positive sometimes.

Love is patient, love is kind. (Something Corinthians. I don't care. I'm not patient, but I'm being as kind as I can be.).

She has a facial tick now that she didn't have a few months ago. She shifts her jaw over and clicks her teeth together. I hate that noise. Because that's not Mom.

My father had a lot of gas powered tools in the garage before he passed, and I knew how to work none of them. I ended up buying lighter-weight cordless variants of many of them, including a leaf blower, which I used almost daily in the fall and spring. At some point this summer, my mother's paranoia inexplicably kicked in, and she started hiding the leaf blower.

Today I was planting flowers in the yard and she mentioned that we used to have a green shovel for planting things. But someone took it. "It disappeared".

I really do try to have patience, but it feels like I cannot get through a day without this exact conversation, just with different objects.

In an attempt to show her that no one took the shovel, I went to look in all the places I thought it would be. Not in the garage. Not in the shop. Not in the basement. Ah, found it. The shovel was in the dining room. She seemed confused, and didn't remember putting it there.

Then I asked her about the leaf blower. She said she'd go get it from the secret place. I pretended to get ice out of the refrigerator so I could see what room she went to (I still don't know exactly where it was.) But she brought it out and said people keep taking it and it's HER blower. I said, well *I* bought it, and *I* use it. And we can't use it if it's hidden all the time.

I couldn't handle having that conversation any longer, so I just left the rest of the gardening for tomorrow and went to the garage apartment. I left the blower with her. Later that night I went to see if I could find the hiding spot for the blower. I opened the door to the china closet, and there was… the shovel.

I gave up and bought another leaf blower and put my name on it with a marker. So now we have two.

61

MOTHER'S DAY

They said that some dementia patients respond really well to art and music because the right side of the brain stays more engaged as the disease progresses. So for Mother's Day, I made a lighted sign with battery powered Christmas lights and cardboard and markers. And I arranged it with a gift in the kitchen, so it would be the first thing she saw when she came downstairs for breakfast.

She came downstairs earlier than usual, and I was still washing dishes. I wished her a Happy Mother's Day. She wandered past me and the blinking marqui cardboard display, because she was trying to find the cat. She saw the blinking lights and the card and gift but was so focused on the cat she didn't stop to look at it at all.

That hurt my feelings. I spent a lot of time trying to make something she'd be really excited about. The important thing to remember is this: It's not about me. It's about her. Go help her find the goddamn cat. Helping her find what she wants right now is the best present, and right now she needs that cat more than a blinking Mother's Day sign on the table.

I'm getting better at it getting worse.

Losing dad was hard but was only ten weeks. Losing mom might take a decade.

This is interfering with my life. No. This is teaching you what's important.

Sometimes I feel bad for not physically coming to the main house to see her a few times a day. But the reality of it is, I think about her all the time. Using the cameras, I check to make sure her lights are on in the morning. If they're on, then she hasn't fallen getting downstairs. She's mobile. Similarly, I can see when the lights go off. I make sure her bills are paid. I make sure her medicines are up to date and in her pill boxes which I sort out late at night when she's asleep. That buys me a month away. I make sure the taxes get paid, the car tags are up to date, her car is washed, the wine is stocked, and so is the chocolate.

I love her.

At the same time, I do not enjoy being around her. It's sad. She has the same conversations over and over. She's accused me of being a thief, a liar, and a slut. She didn't use those words, but that's what she meant.

Life is much easier in the woods, away from her. There, I'm close enough to help her, but far enough away to not have accusations hurled at me when she's having a bad day.

She just called me and asked when I was coming home. She asked if I am mad at her, which broke my heart. Outloud I said, "No, I'm just tired".

I feel guilty for staying away so long. It's been a couple of weeks. She said she misses me. Today she is being sweet.

I miss her too. And unfortunately, the person that's my mom is never coming back. Sure she sometimes has flashes where things seem a little normal. You can't trust that. She might accuse me of being a thief in five minutes if she can't find her kitchen timer.

While I'm at the cabin and she says she misses me, part of me wants to drive back. It's just two hours. But then I remember the ceiling fans, and Wally, and her thinking that I had several men over at the garage apartment at the same time. And with such anger she accused me of sleeping with multiple men that evening "in your daddy's office", and they were coming to the house to take a shower afterward. I explained that Wally needed to take a shower because he'd been working on her ceiling fans all day, and we were going to dinner. And all she could say was an angry, "Well... you need to do better."

I need to do better? Did you WANT to go straight to a nursing home and let me get back to MY life? Did you WANT to have ceiling fans that posed a huge fire hazard? Did you WANT me to focus on my career instead of caring for you? Did you WANT me to let you run out of chocolate and wine? I can leave and go back to California any time and let you fend for yourself.

I realize that I cannot say those things. I have to be the adult here. Saying those things would be cruel and like yelling at a child. But it is really hard to be judged for things you didn't do. It's a sense of injustice that will never be righted. There will never be an apology. You take that bullet and move on. As an adult child acting as caretaker, there is also still a sense of needing approval, at least for me, which is painful when you're doing all you can, and it's not seen.

It's not enough now, and it's never going to be. It is a thankless role. It's less than thankless. Insults, insinuations, accusations. You have to stop caring about those things. You put on your bulletproof empathy vest. Let her talk. Love her anyway. And I know in my heart, I'm doing the best things for her, even if she doesn't see it. It is hard loving a stranger who has flashes of Mom.

Part of my way of coping with loving her now is by not living in her house. I can't help her if I'm losing my mind. I'm taking care of me, so I can take care of her when she needs me.

"Do better?"

There are plenty of things I could do better. Taking care of my mother is not one of them.

62

KAT & SUPERPOWERS

Through a mutual friend, I met Kat. She is super smart, kind, gorgeous, accomplished, a world traveler, funny, and beautifully spiritual.

In 2018, after four months of being away from San Francisco, I was looking forward to seeing my friends, but I didn't get to see Kat. She and her boyfriend broke up on the day that I flew back, and during my layover she texted to ask if she could stay with me. Of course, yes. But not as a long term solution, since I already had my friend Ali staying with me.

Kat has family in San Diego, so she flew there instead of staying with me, but we did catch up on the phone.

A normal breakup is typically difficult emotionally and sometimes logistically. A San Francisco breakup is exponentially more stressful and complicated because of high rents and few options. Even ignoring the logistical components here, Kat was without her man, her home, her dog, her things, her job that she'd just left, and now her city. So much on her suddenly.

Add to that the loss of a future she'd envisioned. She really wanted a partner and a baby, and at 40 she felt pressure to start over quickly.

But at the same time, she wasn't ready to move on in all directions at once immediately. It had just happened. Also, WHAT just happened? Out of nowhere, life got scrambled.

We both cried on the phone while she was explaining this flow of incredible heartache and uncertainty.

If there's anything that losing my dad taught me, it's to not say all those things that people tend to say at times like this. People tend to want to reassure you. "It's going to be OK."

Yeah maybe, but it doesn't FEEL OK NOW!

Kat and I laughed about that for a bit. Cry-laughing.

When my friends are hurting so much, I remember that I would love my superpower to be this: the ability to take on another person's suffering so we could share it, and make it hurt less on the other.

I suppose we all have that superpower, a little.

What I told Kat, was that I promised I wasn't going to try to make her feel better. But I told her the two questions I ask myself which sometimes get me through bad moments.

1) Am I breathing right now? Yes.
2) Am I in physical pain? No.

Then you can do anything. OK...OK... OK.

That seemed to help a little bit. Maybe.

The drawback about those questions is that sometimes we are actually NOT breathing when we're upset. And sometimes in a breakup, there IS physical pain. So my two-question method here is not a perfect solution, but it's a starting point.

Kat did eventually move in with me for a few months, then she found a gloriously beautiful apartment in San Francisco with views for miles and a deck full of sunshine.

And I'm happy to report that Kat is now with a wonderful man who loves to travel the world with her. Losing that boyfriend years ago hurt and necessitated recalibration, but sometimes unfulfilled dreams turn into better realities.

Huge cheers to Kat!

63

LITTLE THINGS

July 4th, 2020 at the cabin was really fun.

Neighbors Martha, Alexander, Jeff, and Jeff's girlfriend Teresa came over. We ate way too much and played badminton. Teresa's hundred pound lovable dog Ana came too. She and Athena get along. We all laughed the whole time outside because we are all terrible at badminton. If anyone had been good at it, we wouldn't have had half as much fun.

It's been two years since Dad died. I don't get sad like I did before. But sometimes I really wish he were here. He would have loved every second of life at the cabin now. He loved being around people. He would have loved the dogs. He would have loved to see people enjoying the cabin he built.

Two years. And I still find things like a bar of soap or a shampoo container that were his. He touched that. It's not like I'm saving it. It's just… it was his. It's funny how something like soap can make you remember someone.

Today I had a dream about Dad. I was driving down the road and saw him in his truck. We got out of our cars and hugged. It seemed so real.

I'm still sorting out how I think about souls and if they come to you after they're gone. I'm not sure it matters if I sort it out or just go with it. What I do know is Dad came to me then, as energy in the universe or through memories, just neurons in my head. I'm thankful for the dream though. I got to hug him there.

64

WAYS TO SHOW LOVE

This week, I've been deep cleaning the house. We used to have a house cleaner, Cecelia, come once or twice a month, but a year ago Mom got upset with her and told her not to come anymore. Normally Cecelia works for four hours, and one day she left after three hours. So she got in trouble for working faster. Mom also thinks she was stealing things like towels. Doubtful.

With all the dust and cobwebs, I tried using the vacuum last week. The handle was duct-taped and floppy. Wires were exposed. Why the heck are we keeping this?! I felt bad that Cecelia ever had to use that dangerous monstrosity.

I threw out the old vacuum and ordered a new one. It came Wednesday. It's now Sunday. So for five days now, I've been vacuuming for hours. There are cobwebs everywhere.

We really need Cecelia. She's probably a lot better at this than I am.

I brought Athena into the house with me today. I was cleaning in the attic. Athena wanted to be with me, even though it was 110' up there. She does NOT want to be with me when I'm using the vacuum though, so I walked her downstairs for the vacuuming phase. I asked

Mom to please not leave the door open when Athena is in the house. Mom sometimes leaves the door open for the cat to come in and out. That's normally fine, but Athena could easily be run over since we live on a busy road, and she's an adventurer.

When I came downstairs from vacuuming in the attic, I looked for Athena. I couldn't find her, and the outside door was open.

I asked where Athena was. Mom didn't know. I said, "Well you let her out... Don't do that."

And she said "I didn't let her out." Obviously she did. She either let her out or gave her the opportunity to let herself out by leaving the door open.

The point is that Mom didn't protect her, even though I specifically asked her not to leave the door open when Athena was in the house.

Then Mom said I should put her on a leash. As if this is MY FAULT that she left the door open. Her brain doesn't work. Her brain doesn't work. Her brain doesn't work. It's not her fault. It's not her fault. Breathe. Breathe. Breathe,

I went outside and screamed for Athena. Eventually she came back.

I cannot trust my mom to take care of anything. The house, the dog, herself.

Mom has called me twice tonight. I didn't answer. I know she is OK, because I can see her walking around. Nothing she says about the dog situation will make sense, and it would likely only make me more angry.

Is Athena more important than being kind to my mom? No. I love my mom. I am also really frustrated. Athena could have gotten very hurt.

Sometimes loving someone is best shown by simply not yelling at them when you really want to.

65

TWO DATES and a FUNERAL

Dating when you're a caretaker can be difficult.

For me, all other relationships were to some extent compromised or put on a soft pause while I was taking care of my parents. It's hard to be on point as an employee, friend, or partner when you're always on high alert at home.

But sometimes I did visit with friends.

One time, a dinner party with old friends ran late, and while I was taking a car service home I received a call from 911.

Fearing the worst, I answered to find that my mom had apparently called the police because I wasn't home by midnight. It was about 12:30. She hadn't called me because she couldn't remember the number, but she somehow found it when she called 911.

She had no reason to be afraid for me that night. I was with good friends.

The next time police were involved, I was not with a friend.

It wasn't supposed to be a date, but that's the best way to describe it.

It was Labor Day 2020, in Birmingham, Alabama. I was taking care of my mom and needed a break. I wanted to play pool.

I met someone on a social media site, and he also liked to play pool. I jokingly said I was really bad at pool, and I looked forward to him beating me. In hindsight, that was a really bad choice of words.

Due to COVID, every pool place was closed, so we met at my house (again, in hindsight, a bad idea), and we walked to my favorite sushi place. We had fun talking for several hours, and we stayed until they closed. We walked back home, and since we'd had drinks, he said he didn't feel safe driving 90 minutes back to his house yet, which I respected as responsible, so I said he could stay as long as he needed to, to be sober.

And all was well. UNTIL HE KICKED Athena.

Ian Disney is my assailant/date.

Athena whimpered, and I immediately and calmly asked Ian to leave. He did. And 45 seconds later he came back, forced his way into the house, and strangled me.

Sometimes people really don't take rejection well.

I want to emphasize that at this point, all he had to do was leave my home. There was nothing to be gained by coming back other than acting out of anger.

Everything that happened after this also makes no sense. And none of it was consensual. I'm omitting the graphic details.

He choked me until I passed out. Many times. At least four times. It's hard to remember events when you've lost oxygen, so it might have been more than four times.

He said he'd tell the police that he'd met some kinky girl who asked for it. I don't remember a lot of this because of the choking, but I had cameras that caught all of the yelling -- all him. So he was already planning to be talking to police, and lie. Also, we were not having sex, and I did not ask for anything other than for him to leave, as is evident from the video footage. I hate to say it this way, but thank GOD my mother had dementia, and to protect HER I'd installed about twenty cameras at our house, which captured him chasing me outside, fully clothed, dragging me around by my hair, and screaming at me.

There was one thing he didn't scream. He whispered: "No one can hear you. No one is coming to save you."

The cameras did not catch that. But I will never forget it.

He was right. No one was coming.

I had to save myself. I fought every way I could. I hit him when he was strangling me. He said I was trying to be an MMA fighter. I still have scars on my hands from hitting him in the mouth. I fought with ALL of my might. I've never hit anyone before in my life. I do lift weights though, and I got two great shots in. I bet he wasn't expecting that. It wasn't enough though. He still choked me out.

At one point he had me sit on the floor and wouldn't let me move. He went on long rants about how American women will "f*** you up". I don't know what that was about. We're both American. I never threatened him once.

I told him I had to go to the bathroom. He strangled me again, and he told me he didn't believe me, so I defecated on him. THAT'S RIGHT!

I pooped on this asshole. He ushered me into the bathroom and watched me finish. Then he took a few seconds to clean himself, and that's when I ran! Unfortunately he caught up with me outside and choked me out again.

I am so lucky to be alive. He said he'd kill me, and I knew he would. He twisted my neck to where I could hear it starting to snap. I'd tried fighting, I'd tried running. He was GOING TO KILL ME. He threatened to shoot me with a gun to my head. So I knew I had to de-escalate. He needed to feel validated and in the right. We are in a realm of all EMOTION. There's no logic left here. I told him I was sorry, and this was my fault. I misunderstood. He was right, and I just misinterpreted. I've heard this called fawning. I fawned the fuck out of this nightmare, and it kept me alive.

He wouldn't let me out of his sight for hours, so I had to "sleep" next to this crazy person, but around 6 am, I said I needed to take care of my mom, which was true. He let me do that. Also, I did not want her to know that there was anything wrong. It would be confusing. It would be confusing for anyone, but especially an 80 year old with dementia. Then again, with dementia, maybe she'd forget, so maybe it wasn't that big of a deal to worry about!. Anyway, I didn't tell her anything about all of this. I wanted the day to feel normal for her, so I didn't call the police. Not yet. But I didn't have to call them. They found me. I'll get there in a second.

Upon leaving, Ian Disney said, "I had a really nice time. I hope to see you again."

To get rid of him, I calmly said "Me too." The Academy Awards committee can send me the Oscar statue whenever they're ready.

Like many people who are just thankful to be alive, I didn't call the police. I called my best friend and my neighbor. My friends really helped me over months.

Guess who physically went to the police immediately. This jerk got himself arrested based on what HE SAID to them describing what had happened. They arrested him on domestic violence charges. I didn't pursue that, because to me, that wasn't strong enough.

The police came to my house an hour later. They sent four men to take pictures of my house and my body.

FOUR. MEN. MY. BODY.

They couldn't find a female officer?!!! For a woman just assaulted. That's shameful.

There were physical ramifications. The bruises healed quickly. But I could not sit up on my own for two weeks because of how hard I fought. My core muscles were exhausted. Also, I couldn't speak normally for about two months because he damaged my vocal cords. And the whites of my eyes were solid blood.

Visine didn't help me out of this one. You just have to look like you might have ebola for about two months.

The emotional damage was worse though.

I was absolutely terrified of him. He knew where I lived. He'd threatened to kill me with obvious intent and obvious enjoyment of almost killing me many times.

I pressed charges. Based on the pictures and video, the DA arrested him on Attempted Murder,

Kidnapping, Rape, and Burglary. I think they could have added a few more, but that sentence was probably going to be life anyway. (In case you're interested, Burglary doesn't mean they stole something, it just means they came into a place where they were not welcome.)

Bond was $240k, and you only have to pay the court 10% of the bond amount to get out (I hate that I now know this), but he came up with $24k in cash in a day. So my thinking at this point is this: All I did last time was ask him to leave my house and he lost it. And now there are serious legal charges against him, and he's free. So what's he going to do now? My guess is KILL US. He already said he was going to.

We have to leave.

I moved my mother to a retirement community, and I went into hiding at the cabin in the woods. Both of us out of reach. Thank you to my dad. Thank you for that cabin.

Two months later, a social worker called me.

Ian Disney is dead. They did not give me details other than to say that they had to use multiple ways of identifying him and that he was in a plane at the time. He was a pilot.

I burst into tears. I'm not sure why I cried. I think it was a combination of relief for myself, compassion for the family, and lament for the senselessness of it all.

It didn't have to happen. He could have just left my house. Instead he chose to hurt me. The PTSD from this is still with me.

Just after he left my house, he texted, "I hope this doesn't make you hate men." I quickly responded, "Oh I don't hate men. You're not a MAN."

The happy news is that three days before all of this, I met a wonderful man, Ken, who helped me and is now my boyfriend. After just three days of knowing me, he sat with me in the emergency room until three a.m. We've been dating for many years now. And Athena the dog sleeps on HIS feet (traitor). ;)

One of the ways he was wonderful right from the start was that when I told him if he wanted to go on a date with me, he had to meet my mom first, so he'd know why I always answer calls, and I don't leave her. He brought roses and wine, because I told him she liked to have wine outside in the afternoon, if it's nice. She likes to be inside by six p.m for Wheel of Fortune.

Ken also brought his new guitar and made up a song for my mom called "Dottie" (her name). He was really bad, which made it even better. We all laughed.

Ken worked at a hospital close by. Unfortunately Mom eventually did fall and end up in the hospital, and because of COVID restrictions I couldn't see her much. But as an administrator, Ken could visit her regularly, and he did. He was a godsend.

Another happy point around this time is, my mom kept talking about a party that we had to get ready for. With dementia patients you just go with it.

It's almost like improv's rule of "yes... and".

I'm asking things like: "So yeah, where's that party?", "How should we dress?", "Who's going?"

She wasn't sure, but there was definitely a party and many people are coming. I asked her who, and she gestured to all the people in the room, and she made eye contact with them.

The thing is, there was no one there.

She was seeing something I couldn't see. I truly believe she saw souls that were with her somehow. We were in a hospital then. You don't have to tell me twice to have a party, especially if ghosts are invited. It was on!

Mom came home, shortly after this.

I love Halloween. I invited everyone we knew. And WE. HAD. A. PARTY.

Mom came as a queen with a tiara and a cape. We burned a piano in the back yard. Note: It was completely broken, so no functional pianos were harmed in the making of this party.

We danced, sang, and laughed until the wee hours.

My mom died ten days later. I held her hand and told her it was ok to go. I'd heard that sometimes a person at the bridge needs to feel permission to leave. After our conversation she died peacefully just hours later.

She sure got her party though! :)

And Athena was at her side until the very end. She knew.

66

MOM'S NEXT ADVENTURE

Mom died November 9th, 2021. The death certificate says it was November 10th. That is because these things are recorded according to someone who was not there.

I didn't want my mom to die. But, at some point, she wasn't really living.

She didn't want her wine at four p.m. anymore. She didn't want to watch Wheel of Fortune. She didn't even want snickers and oreos. She left this earth peacefully though.

This is what I said at Mom's funeral:

******

I am Natalie Haynes, the daughter of Dottie Haynes and Joe Haynes.

Thank you for being here.

...

Love is patient, love is kind...

That verse from Corinthians always reminds me of my mom.

She was so patient.

She had to be patient to put up with me and my dad. We were a handful.

She really was a shining example of love in action.

Mom was beautiful inside and out. A devoted and supportive wife. A teacher, an artist, a great mother, and a wonderful cook.

Mom was creative and smart.

One of my first memories with her is my sitting under the dining room table and drawing while she painted above me.

In talking with others, my mother downplayed her strengths, but she was undoubtedly the glue of our family. We didn't have a lot of conflict, but if there was ever discord, she brought the peace.

Some people lead softly, wisely. She was like that. She taught me that there is powerful strength in acts of patience and kindness.

As members of this church for over 40 years, my parents are known to many of you very well, but I'd like to share a few aspects of my mother that you may not have heard about before.

My mother had an independent adventurous spirit. We traveled together many times. And she enjoyed trying new things.

Mom was fun. She was also very devoted to the church. In 2009, I asked her to go to Puerto Rico with me on a Monday, and she said she couldn't go because she had Bible study on Wednesday.

I convinced her that it would be ok to miss one week of Bible study. So we went to Puerto Rico, and one night we ended up paddling up a creek alone in pitch black darkness in a kayak, because we got separated from our tour group. The tour was to see a special lagoon that lit up when you paddled, so you can only go at night. I had planned to go on this kayak adventure on my own, but Mom wanted to go. I intended to do all of the paddling for us, but when we got separated from our group, I needed her help because we couldn't see anything, and we got stuck every time the creek turned.

In the dark, we kept paddling together. We made it work.

And we giggled the whole time. It was scary, but it was funny, and it felt ok because we had each other.

I was glad I had her on my team that night.

I am glad I've had her on my team always.

Since my father passed in 2018, life has felt a lot like that -- making it work, giggling at times even if it's scary, and glad that we have a team.

Mom's spirit is sweet. It is also strong.

I read something once saying that the strongest trees are the ones that bend when the wind blows hard. Those are the ones that don't break.

My mother was definitely resilient.

She was also positive and brave. A few years ago she needed a serious surgery, and when I walked in the hospital to see her, she proudly showed me how she'd organized all the tubes coming out of her using the safety pins she had in her purse. Of course she did. Ever the hostess, she also offered me saltines.

Earlier, I said that my mom's spirit is strong. I say that in present tense, because her faith was clear. When my father died, Mom told me that she looked forward to being with him in heaven. Departing OUR presence physically is not an ending for her.

Theirs was a deep love. Or rather it IS a deep love.

I think we can all keep loving her as she was, as she is.

Two more things I'd like to say:

1) Thank you to the wonderful women who have helped my mom in the last months: Ashaki, Myeisha, Evelyn, and Vette. THEY are the real wonder women here.
2) I'd like to read the full set of verses from 1st Corinthians, chapter 13, verses 4-8.

A few years ago, I had this etched on the inside of bracelets for my mother and for me. Having both on today makes me feel like Wonder Woman with a ROAR OF LOVE from all of our hearts. Everyone here, and everyone who wanted to be.

4 Love is patient, love is kind. It does not envy, it does not boast, it is not proud. 5 It is not rude, it is not self-seeking, it is not easily angered, it keeps no record of wrongs. 6 Love does not delight in evil but rejoices with the truth. 7 It always protects, always trusts, always hopes, always perseveres.

That is Dottie Haynes to me. Amen.

67

THE PHONE BOOTH
AND THE DANCE

There was a tsunami in Japan in 2011. A man who lost his cousin put an old disconnected rotary phone in a phone booth at the edge of his garden in his yard so he could have a place to talk to his cousin. Eventually others came to the "Wind Phone" in their grief as well, wanting to talk with their loved ones who had also passed. Some of them came with tears. Some came with matter of fact details about their lives as if they were just catching up.

Listening to a radio show about the phone booth reminded me of Burningman. In case you haven't heard of it, it's a huge art and music festival in the middle of the Nevada desert with beautiful displays of creativity, music, and art.

Some people are familiar with the wooden man that burns. What many people don't know about is the temple. The temple is much bigger than the wooden man that burns. Like the man that burns, the temple is a temporary wooden structure that's built every year, then burns, and then is rebuilt the next year.

During the week leading up to "the burn" you can visit the temple, walk around inside, pray, meditate, leave notes, leave writings, leave pictures. It is a somber place for quiet, reflection, and recognition of loss and things that people need to let go of. There are pictures of lost parents, partners, children, friends, pets. There are also joyful celebratory expressions. It is simply a place to bare your heart.

People come from all over the world, so the expressions are in many languages.

I visited once. While I was there, one man started what I can only describe as a tribal dance. He sang in a language I do not know, other than it was pain. He wailed as he danced. I have no idea what words he said, but I do know what he felt. It is the most moving raw true human expression of sorrow that I have ever seen. He yelled. He stomped. He got down on his knees and raised his hands and crying face to the sky. It was a dance-prayer.

It was beautiful. I'm glad he shared it. It is still with me.

68

REACHING OUT FOR HELP

I am stubborn and independent, but losing my dad gave me a new level of humility and gratitude. I started asking for help. And then with the attack, my whole world changed, and I needed help very often. I needed someone with me constantly either in person or on the phone, even when I slept. The PTSD from that experience was immense. The ensuing support I had was also immense. My friends and family really showed up for me. I can't list every person here, because we'd need 50 pages, but just a few from day 1: Jeff, Athena's dad, immediately drove two hours to see me and gave me a gun holster. My cousin Maggie, an ER doctor, came to the house to check my injuries, and she insisted that I go to the hospital. My friend Catherine, took one of her "work from home" days to work at my house, so I wouldn't be alone. She also helped take pictures of my injuries. My neighbor Helen sat with me, and she tried to help me think through what to do legally. Friends I hadn't talked with in decades called me. My net was strong and powerful.

When I think of that net that catches me now, I recognize which strands in the net were made of steel.

Now after a few years, I'm mostly beyond the PTSD. My intention is to be part of the net of steel that catches my loved ones when they feel like they are falling.

69

MARC O. AMAGALLON

If you thought anything I've said so far was sweet, let me assure you, I'm not always sweet, and Marc O. Amagallon will undoubtedly agree. He is not the steel part of the net that caught me. He is the toilet paper that I got off of my shoes.

I met Marc at the gym. He was nice to me when some other guy was rude to me and took the bench press I'd already set up. Marc saw this and offered that I could use the bench he was using. That started a friendship. We talked a lot there, and then he found me online and emailed me. Then he asked me out for drinks. On one of our first dates, I asked if he had a roommate, and he said no. Then he came to my house. He kissed me. He built my bed. He picked me up and carried me to it.

At some point he told me he lived with a girlfriend. She had cancer, so he couldn't leave her right now. He couldn't remember the last time they had sex. Several months later he said leaving her would be a seven-figure problem. I should have stopped right there.

But he brought me flowers often and said he loved me, and I believed him.

We met before work, during work, and after work. Hundreds of times. Sometimes just for coffee. Usually not for coffee.

One of the texts: "I will have you after the gym tonight."

This level of flirting went on for FOUR years. We had so much fun together. Aside from the obvious, we went to art museums, dinners, hiking trails, dog walks, parties at the beach. Everything a boyfriend would be. Almost.

One afternoon, he said I was like a vacation. He meant it as a compliment, but even then I thought "I'm not a vacation. I'm a real person."

I was ignoring all the red flags.

And then when my dad got sick, I started staying in Birmingham more. Marc didn't want to talk with me when I was there except for a few calls. The last explicit call was July 2020. I was attacked just weeks later in September. And Marc didn't call me for TWO MONTHS after I'd texted that I'd been badly hurt. I'm still incredulous that someone could ignore such hurt in a friend, and being that callous to someone you professed to LOVE. I wasn't trying to date him at that point. I was legitimately just healing. Taking care of my mom, the house, legal issues, and starting therapy because I was so scared of Ian Disney. That experience upended my life. I needed my friends, and I thought Marc was one.

Now I see that if I wasn't the hot girl at the gym, then we're not even humans that interact. Six weeks prior, he was fine having a detailed, explicit conversation, asking me for photos of my body (I sent one fully clothed at the gym). He sent me a picture of his crotch. And when I actually needed something important, like a caring friend, he's not there. He later said he was "out of range".

Don't worry, it gets better.

My therapist told me to write about this. I did.

So my attack was in September. In December, I was at the cabin with limited paper supplies. I had postcards. I wrote what I wanted to say on six postcards, which I mailed all at once. I'll get to those.

Later, he said I was malicious because I wrote them so anyone could read them. That is not true. My intent was not malicious. I was simply ambivalent about the consequences. And I saw no need to protect him. My body had been beaten, and he seemed to only care about my body when he could use it. He doesn't care about me. I don't see a need to take care regarding him.

Also, technicaly it's illegal to read someone else's mail. Unless you make it into artwork, such as a book. So here we are:

Postcard 1

> I am channeling a lot of anger towards you, because you treated me like trash and Kate too. I can easily let you go, but I'm angry, so I'm going to talk now and say the exact truth. Slowly.

> "Out of range". Bullshit. CAN YOU HEAR ME NOW?

> When a friend is hurt, you find a way to be in range. I'm so angry because, 4 years, Marc.

Postcard 2

> Here's our problem: You don't communicate, so I'll communicate.

> I wasn't asking for anything from you except a phone call. After the attack, I couldn't be alone for about a month. Every

single one of my exes and friends helped me by being on the phone or sitting in person, even while I slept. He was going to KILL me, and my mom and dog. How is it that everyone else helped me and you didn't. Your excuse: You didn't give a fuck.

Postcard 3

Four years of you lying to Kate. I asked you to tell her. Like I said, you make it easy to not be jealous of her because I know what she's sleeping next to. When someone almost killed me, you couldn't call me because you were in and out of service, for a week, and then two more months went by.

The mail is in service.

Postcard 4

You told me some of your ex-lovers acted crazy. Maybe you just didn't treat them very nicely. Call me crazy if you wish.

You can throw arrows at the sun. It still shines as bright.

You called me "Match Girl". Well, I'm solidly burning this bridge.

Postcard 5

I didn't expect you to be in love with me. I just expected you to treat me like a human when I really needed good friends to help me and just to talk with. We have been friends for YEARS and you were not there. Not at all. You sent flowers twice when my dad was sick. This was worse than my dad's death. Someone tried to kill me. I gathered every ounce of strength I had to fight this guy, and then I pulled together every person that cared about me to help me through the aftermath. To say you only had three minutes to talk before your doctor's appointment – that's just an insult.

Postcard 6

You couldn't make the time to call me when someone strangled me and was charged with attempted murder, kidnapping, and rape. You had no regard for my life as I knew it. I do not feel compelled to protect yours anymore either. That is not a threat. I am just sending words. All true.

After this recent incident my doctor encouraged me to write. So I'm writing. Again, all truth. I'll start small here. It seems like you only like to talk to me when you have the opportunity to fuck me. Noted. You did say, "Sex with you is like nothing else." I'm not sure if that was a compliment.

I hope Jett (dog) is doing ok. I hope the racoons are staying outside. I hope the girls in Oakland are taking care of the house and that those trees in the back are not growing through the windows.

Merry Christmas

THAT is a solid way to lose someone.

It's easy to write his behavior off as "he's just not that into you – anymore". Sure. Fine. But that isn't what it was about. I wasn't trying to date him. I was reaching out as a very hurt human, and he didn't care.

It seemed to me like a baffling callous betrayal of humanity.

It's like seeing someone hit by a car, when they are gasping for breath, and not stopping to help.

He saw a bad collision and passed right by.

His damage to me was as bad as Ian Disney's.

I truly feel sorry for Kate. He lied to me – about me. He lied to me – about her. I'm sure he lied to her about me. Lies. Lies. Lies.

Thankfully I have a host of better friends.

I sent these six postcards not knowing if Marc still had a girlfriend or if she was even still alive. Apparently, she was alive and got the postcards before he did. She messaged me online. She asked to talk.

We chatted via text one night. I really didn't want to hurt her further, so I answered with 100% truth, but I was very measured. I wanted to say SO much more. I wanted to scream that he said it was a "SEVEN FIGURE PROBLEM" to leave her. RUN! She makes more than he does. I was probably not the only one! I wanted to tell her to get screened for STDs. But that really wasn't my place. So I just answered what she wanted to know.

I wish her well. And I hope she's found someone better by now.

70

THE REASONS,
THE BLESSINGS

My friend Martha says it all the time: "Everything happens for a reason." And as I said earlier, I just don't think that's true.

But I do think one can almost always find a way to be grateful, even in the face of negative things. And that brings me to Alexander's story.

Alexander lost his parents before he even had them. As a newborn, they didn't take care of him (not changing his diaper, burn marks on his feet, not having a proper place to sleep). Martha, who is Alexander's great grandmother and her husband Griff rescued him from the squalor and emotional abuse that was already happening at five weeks old. They officially adopted him as their son, and he was welcomed into a beautiful, kind, loving, household.

As of this writing, he's sixteen, around 6 feet tall already, and has a wild mane of red hair. He's a strong, smart, handsome, hard-working, kind, polite, young man. He loves animals, music, and fixing things. He's doing very well. I doubt he'd have done so well with those first parents.

Griff passed away about nine years ago, so it's just been Alexander and Martha, plus the fifteen dogs, seven cats, and the chickens since then.

One day on the phone, Martha asked if I'd be Alexander's godmother. Of course, yes! She's in her 70's so she's just worried about what will happen for Alexander if something happens to her.

A decade ago, I lost two babies, and now after 40 I don't want to try to get pregnant. But being a godmother is perfect. We're training for a half-marathon together.

If I'd had my first child, he would be Alexander's age now.

When I didn't have children, that created so many blessings than I'm thankful for. If I'd had children, I wouldn't have had time to take care of my parents when they needed me most.

So on to questioning "What is the reason?" I'm going to shift to using the word blessing instead of reason.

The biggest blessing of my dad dying when he did is that he didn't have to witness and handle my mom's decline. He loved her so much, and she was sliding away, which would have broken his heart. And if he'd been around for the Ian Disney incident where I was hurt, Dad would very possibly have killed him and gone to prison. I'm glad Dad went before both of those things.

Where is the blessing in losing Mom? These really don't feel like blessings, but she and the dementia taught me a deeper level of both patience and compassion.

My choices during the decline of Dad and Mom showed me what my priorities were and are. The equation of my life became more clear in terms of which variables matter and how heavy the coefficients are.

Showing love for my family, friends, and partner have become much more important than ever before.

My short list of other life variables: I always want flowers on my table, my chainsaw, my dog.

I also now have two businesses. Art and data analytics.

I happily do both, and I'm constantly reminded that a few years ago after a couple of glasses of wine, my dad told me that my greatest gift as a child was art, but they didn't want me to be poor so they made me do more math.

I did like math, and I was eventually the president of the math team in high school. But my initial interest in the math team was less about math and more because I had a crush on one of the boys on the math team. Actually, it was several boys. I married one.

Dad was probably right to guide me towards more profitable waters, but my heart has always leaned toward the creative. I'm thankful that our house in Alabama was always one of creativity and colorful messes.

So back to the reasons.

Why did Ian Disney attack me and later kill himself? Is there anything to learn or to be grateful for here?

The only things I tell myself that remotely help here are, I'm glad he attacked ME, because I'm stubborn and strong, and someone else might not have been. He is dead and can't hurt someone else or me, or my dog, again.

Also, because of that experience, I got to see that my now partner, Ken, was an incredibly nice person. He saw me through dark moments. He told me I was beautiful every day, even when I was severely bruised and had blood in my eyes for months.

In dealing with what happened, I also felt a soft hurricane of beautiful friendships while people listened to me, helped me, and guided me out of years of that trauma. I already knew I had friends, but I know now, I have UNBELIEVABLE friends... and potential accomplices.

My friends at the cabin helped me tremendously.

The only reason I initially went to the cabin was to clean it, stage it, and sell it. If my dad were still alive, I wouldn't have done that, and I wouldn't have met Martha, Jeff, Alexander, Athena, and all the rest of the animals when I did.

I wish I'd spent more time at the cabin when Dad was around, because apparently, as a five year old, Alexander liked to sneak over to the cabin to spend time with my dad while Dad was building it. They worked on projects, talked, and ate cookies.

I didn't meet Alexander until he was 12. But I'm very happy to be his godmother, and maybe Martha is right. Maybe at least sometimes things do happen for a reason.

71

MESSAGE FROM A FRIEND

Nasim and I worked together for five years at the Gap Inc. corporate offices in San Francisco.

Sometimes people dance around a difficult topic or avoid it. I absolutely love that Nasim just outright addressed the elephant in the room when my mother passed.

Sending you prayers Natalie! I'm glad you & your mom were able to spend her last days together.

This is one of my favorite quotations about physical death:

"To consider that after the death of the body the spirit perishes is like imagining that a bird in a cage will be destroyed if the cage is broken, though the bird has nothing to fear from the destruction of the cage. Our body is like the cage, and the spirit is like the bird...if the cage becomes broken, the bird will continue and exist. Its feelings will be even more powerful, its perceptions greater, and its happiness increased..."
- Abdu'l-Baha"

I love this and 100% believe that it is true. In the physical world, if you burn something, it changes physically, but all the pieces, atoms, molecules, whatever we want to call it, they still stay, just not in the same form. Ice melting is a good example of this idea too. It still exists, just in a different form.

This is my favorite thought in framing how to think about losing someone. I've found it helpful when thinking about physical loss and also friendships that didn't endure.

It's OK to lose someone. And sometimes, there is still a beautiful in the awful.

Milton Keynes UK
Ingram Content Group UK Ltd.
UKHW040646110823
426718UK00001B/110

9 798218 956653